MATTHEW'S STORY
Good News for Uncertain Times

William G. Thompson, S.J.

Paulist Press
New York/Mahwah

Special thanks to Bo Svensson for permission to use his photography.

Book design: Ellen Whitney

Library of Congress Cataloging-in-Publication Data

Thompson, William G., 1930–
    Matthew's story : good news for uncertain times / William G. Thompson
      p. cm.
    Bibliography: p.

    ISBN 0-8091-3077-7 : $7.95 (est.)
    1. Bible. N.T. Matthew—Textbooks. I. Title.
BS2575.5.T48   1989   89-9286
226.2′061—dc20   CIP

Published by Paulist Press
997 Macarthur Boulevard
Mahwah, NJ 07430

Printed and bound in the
United States of America

Table of Contents

*Dedicated to My Companions in
the Society of Jesus*

Prologue

Welcome to Matthew's gospel—a story, a narrative, a tale! It is about Jesus and John the Baptist, about Jesus' followers, about people who ask to be cured, about crowds who flock to him, and about his enemies—the Jewish and Roman authorities. The gospel includes five speeches in which Jesus teaches about the reign of God.

We call Matthew's story "good news," a gospel, because it proclaims the reign of God—God's powerful, faithful love for the world. That love is revealed in the world through the words and actions of Jesus of Nazareth. He preaches the good news, teaches in synagogues, heals disease and casts out demons, tells simple stories from everyday life, argues with his enemies, suffers and dies, but is raised to new life. He will come again in glory. Jesus' words and actions disclose how God's power works in our world and how it will be revealed at the end of the age.

I want to share with you the story about Matthew's story about Jesus of Nazareth. I know the story well. At the Biblical Institute in Rome, I studied Matthew's gospel as a document dating to the earliest days of Christianity. I learned how the story was written in response to the needs of a Christian community in their uncertain times. I published my doctoral dissertation as a book entitled

Matthew's Advice to a Divided Community—Mt 17:22–18:35 (Biblical Institute Press, 1970). In addition, I also published articles in several magazines for biblical scholars.

For the past twenty years, I have worked with adults whose interest in Matthew differs from the interest I developed in doctoral studies. With these adults I now ask how Matthew's gospel might speak to us in our own uncertain times, how it might enrich our approach to lives today as individuals and communities as well as our relationship with God. Through my teaching experience I have found a way of looking at this story that respects both what the gospel meant to Matthew and his community and what it can mean to us today as the word of God. Now I want to tell you the story about Matthew's story, about the good news it provides as a guide for us in meeting the challenges of our uncertain times.

You may have read Matthew's story of Jesus or heard excerpts of it in church. Now I will describe its origins, its plot and characters, and the man who wrote it. I invite you to read Matthew's gospel as a story and use it for prayer. I will also walk with you through each chapter of Matthew's story and invite you to reflect on the truth and meaning it carries. I will conclude by describing the good news about God and the world that the story announces, the values it teaches, the shape it can give to our lives.

I gladly acknowledge scholars whose research and publication have influenced my view of Matthew's gospel, especially, Raymond E. Brown, Joseph A. Fitzmyer, Donald Senior, Daniel J. Harrington, John P. Meier, Jack Dean Kingsbury, H. Lamar Cope, Richard A. Edwards, Frank J. Matera, and Ronald D. Witherup.

I also acknowledge all those who helped me shape the book, especially my editor, Dolores Ready; also George Connolly, John T. Dillon, S.J., Peter Gilmour, Mary

Sharon Riley, R.C., and the adults to whom I have taught this material.

Finally, I dedicate this book to my companions in the Society of Jesus, especially to Ignatius Loyola and Pedro Arrupe; to the men who formed me in Ignatian spirituality and trained me in philosophy, theology, and sacred scripture; and to Jesuit friends and colleagues throughout the world both living and dead.

PART 1

Describing
Matthew's Story

This first section creates a background for understanding and accepting Matthew's gospel that blends pertinent historical and literary information with our Christian faith. After describing the uncertain times in which Matthew wrote his story about Jesus of Nazareth, I relate those times to our own uncertain times (Chapter 1). Next, I invite you to read Matthew's story with careful attention to its narrative world—its setting in time and place, its plot and characters, its five discourses, and its overall movement (Chapter 2).

Chapter 3 suggests that you pray with Matthew's gospel. Here I recall some methods suited to praying with stories. Finally, I ask Matthew the evangelist to describe the process by which he produced this story about Jesus (Chapter 4). I hope that you will come to appreciate this story as the word of God shared by Matthew and his community in their uncertain times and received by us in our own uncertain times.

Before we begin, I suggest that you reflect on your experience of Matthew's gospel:

When and where have you encountered Matthew's gospel in the past? Not at all? In your personal reading or prayer? In a workshop or course? In worship with your community or in a private retreat?

Write down as many particular experiences as possible. Were they positive experiences? What made them positive? Were they negative experiences? What made them negative?

Complete the following sentence: "At this moment my relationship to Matthew's story about Jesus is best described as . . ."

1

Matthew's World and Ours

Father Gregory Schaffer, a missionary serving in Guatemala, was returning to the diocese of New Ulm, Minnesota for a short visit. The night before his flight he was driving from his village to Guatemala City, so that he could board the airplane early the next morning.

As he drove down the twisting mountain road, he saw in the distance an elderly peasant woman carrying a pot on her head, as Mayan Indian women do in Guatemala. Suddenly she stumbled. Falling off her head and tumbling to the ground, the pot smashed into pieces. Its contents spilled onto the earth. She bent over to pluck the individual grains of corn from the dust and carefully stored them in her shawl. Tears ran down her wrinkled cheeks. The priest stopped to help her. When they had picked up the grain, he continued driving to Guatemala City.

Early the next morning Father Greg took the airplane to the States and that afternoon landed in Minneapolis. Obtaining a car from a friend, he drove west toward New Ulm. As he drove through a small town, he saw a rich, plentiful harvest of corn. Storage elevators were already so full that farmers had to pile their surplus corn on an empty lot across the street. Corn spilled out onto the highway. Cars swerved to miss crushing the golden grains. Some drivers chose to run over the kernels.

Father Greg remembered the elderly Mayan woman he had seen the day before on his way to Guatemala City. To her, individual grains of corn are a staple, as precious as life itself. But to the American drivers, abundant corn is a nuisance on the road. Father Greg was struck by the contrast.

Most Rev. Raymond A. Lucker
Bishop of New Ulm

We live in uncertain times, and we ask troubling questions. Why can we not bridge the gap between grain-poor Guatemala and the grain-rich United States? Why does hunger plague half the planet's people? Why do we lack systems to distribute our food to the rest of the world? Why do hunger, homelessness, and disease stalk not only Guatemala but also the United States?

Why is family life more unstable? Why do both parents often need to work? Why are drugs more available even to young children? Why is the divorce rate increasing? Why is making a permanent commitment so difficult for some married couples? Why are health-care systems shaky? Why can more and more people not afford them? Why can research teams not find cures for AIDS, Alzheimer's, and cancer?

Why are jobs less secure? Why do business managers often replace people with machines? Why must we retire early? Why does unemployment threaten workers? Why cannot laws regulate how we use our environment? Why can we not control toxic waste, acid rain, radioactivity, and the loss of topsoil and forestland? Why can we not find solutions to worldwide terrorism, struggles within nations and between nations, violence on television and in sports events? Why are small systems like families and huge systems like international banking no longer able to provide food and shelter, steady income and health care, a clean and safe environment?

Problems distress us: How can we secure adequate food and housing for all people, quality education for our children, clear air and water, and a healthy, safe environment? Why can we not walk city streets at night alone, get the job we would like to have, trust our elected officials, control the economy? We sense that our world is changing and that we possess little power to determine its direction. But other people have experienced uncertain times. Let us look at one of those times and at a few of those people.

> Simeon ben Eliezer, a Jewish member of the Christian community in Antioch, spent a month with his family in a village forty miles southeast of that major city in Syria. With them he recalled how in A.D. 70 Rome ended the Jewish revolt that Jews in Palestine had started in A.D. 66. Roman armies destroyed the Jewish temple and their sacred city of Jerusalem. Since then Rome had forced Simeon's family to pay heavier taxes and to live with fear of further violence. Gathering each sabbath in their local synagogue, they listened to readings from the Jewish law, reflected on their meaning, and prayed for grace to survive their ordeal and meet their challenges with courage.
>
> When Simeon returned to Antioch, he found his community anxious and troubled. Word had

been received that the Pharisees at Jamnia in Palestine had ordered pressure put on Christian Jews, so that they would withdraw from active membership in their Jewish synagogues. As part of the Pharisees' plan to rebuild Judaism after the tragic revolt against Rome (A.D. 66–70), all Christian-Jews were gradually to be banned from participating in synagogue activities.

Simeon wondered whether this decree from Jamnia would reach the Jewish synagogue in Antioch. Nero, the Roman emperor, had already terrified the Christian community by putting Christians to death in Rome (A.D. 67–69). Peter and Paul were among the martyrs. Christians throughout the Roman empire shared a fear that their lives might also be in danger. Must Simeon now also dread persecution from his fellow Jews? Would these pressures force him to choose between his Jewish family and his Christian community? He often lay awake long into the night troubled by these questions.

Christians, like Simeon ben Eliezer and the members of his community in Antioch, lived in uncertain times. Unrest in both Palestine and Rome caused their insecurity. Jews in Palestine had revolted against Rome in A.D. 66. That revolt ended with Roman armies burning Jerusalem and the Jewish temple in A.D. 70. Before that event Jews held widely different convictions about worshiping in the temple and about observing the Jewish law. Judaism had allowed a wide pluralism of views that included Sadducees and Pharisees and the Essene community outside Jerusalem, as well as movements like the Zealots and the Jews who believed that Jesus of Nazareth was the long-awaited

Messiah. Christianity began as one movement among many movements within Judaism.

Sadducees included aristocratic landowners and priests responsible for the temple worship in Jerusalem. Practical men who were eager to maintain their high social standing, the Sadducees accommodated temple rituals to meet the demands of the Roman leaders who had political power in Palestine. In reaction to Rome's influence on their religious life, the Essenes left Jerusalem to form isolated communities on the northwest shore of the Dead Sea near Qumran. They dedicated themselves to living the Jewish law in its purity until they could unite their efforts to those of the expected Messiah in a battle to restore authentic priesthood and worship to the temple in Jerusalem.

Pharisees steered a middle course between the more accommodating Sadducees and the more reactionary Essenes. Like the Essenes, they rejected the Sadducees' compromise with Rome. But the Pharisees also adapted the Jewish law, so that Jews throughout Palestine could observe it in their everyday lives. With their extensive oral traditions, the Pharisees moved beyond blind adherence to the letter of the law and avoided a literal, legalistic interpretation. Their broader understanding won respect from the Jewish people outside Jerusalem, and their influence spread to synagogues throughout Palestine.

Since Christianity began as a movement within Judaism, Jews who believed Jesus of Nazareth to be their long-awaited Messiah continued to consider themselves still united to their fellow Jews. Their community in Jerusalem, founded by Jesus of Nazareth, claimed Peter and the twelve apostles as authentic witnesses to his words and actions. They had followed Jesus during his life on earth and experienced him as their risen Lord. James, the

brother of the Lord, led the Jerusalem community, while
Peter served as their principal preacher, spokesman, and
missionary. Members shared their goods in common, wor-
shiped at the temple, observed the Jewish law, and broke
bread together in their homes to keep alive their memories
of Jesus (Acts 2:44–47).

After Stephen was put to death, Jews began to persecute the Christian community in Jerusalem. Saul the
Pharisee was empowered to enter homes to drag Christian-Jews, both men and women, off to prison (Acts 8:1–3).
To avoid this persecution, most Christian-Jews left Jerusalem and scattered throughout Palestine. But their
leaders remained in Jerusalem. James was martyred in
A.D. 60.

Fugitives from persecution in Jerusalem founded the
Christian community in Antioch, a city north of Jerusalem
on the Mediterranean Sea in the Roman province of Syria.
This new community soon became second in importance to
the small community that remained in Jerusalem. Antioch
was probably the first community to welcome Gentiles.
Moreover, in Antioch the disciples of the risen Lord were
called Christians for the first time (Acts 11:26).

Saul the Pharisee was on his way to persecute the
Christian-Jews in Damascus when he experienced the
risen Lord. He became Paul—the missionary of Jesus
Christ to the Gentiles. Paul later made Antioch the home
base for his missionary activities. With his co-workers, he
traveled from Antioch to cities in Asia Minor, Macedonia,
and Greece. When Paul preached his message about Jesus
Christ to his fellow Jews in their synagogue, some seemed
interested. But when most grew hostile, Paul moved out of
the Jewish synagogue to a nearby home, where he could
explain his message to both Jews and Gentiles. He orga-
nized home-based communities that included both Jews
and Gentiles.

Paul's success with the Gentiles raised questions for Christians both in Antioch and in Jerusalem: Was their movement meant to include both Jews and Gentiles? If so, must Gentiles become Jews to become Christians? Like Christian-Jews, must they be circumcised and observe the Jewish law? At one point Christian Jews from Jerusalem came to Antioch and taught that salvation for both Jews and Gentiles demanded that they be circumcised and observe the Jewish law. Paul returned to Antioch to find the community deeply divided over the Jew-Gentile issue. He and Barnabas traveled to Jerusalem to resolve the conflict at a council with the leaders in Jerusalem around A.D. 49 (Acts 15).

Within Palestine, activists called Zealots saw themselves as chosen instruments through whom God would deliver the Jewish people from Roman domination. From the time of the return from exile in Babylon (538 B.C.) most Jews in Palestine resented living under Persian, Greek, or Roman political rule. God was their true ruler and king. The Zealots fired the imaginations of their fellow Jews and convinced them that God would support them in a fight against Rome as God had fought with their ancestors in their successful revolt against the Greeks (160–134 B.C.). Zealots promised the Jews that God's support would assure victory and establish them as a free nation under God's exclusive reign. Rome would no longer stand between the Jewish people and their God.

After some preliminary abortive attempts to rid their land of the Romans, the Jews in Palestine began a general revolt in A.D. 66. Jews fought with courage against the powerful Roman legion. But the Romans slowly broke down their resistance in the countryside throughout Galilee and around Jerusalem in Judea. Vespasian led the Roman legions until he was named emperor in A.D. 69. Titus, his son, succeeded Vespasian. After four years of unsuccessful siege, Roman troops finally entered the sacred city of Jerusalem, despoiled the temple, carried off its sacred treasures, and burned both the city and the temple. The Jewish revolt ended with this disaster in A.D. 70. This event marked the end of the restoration that had begun in 538 B.C., when Jews returned from exile to begin rebuilding the temple on Mount Zion in Jerusalem.

David had set the ark of the covenant on Mount Zion, and Solomon had built on that spot a magnificent temple to their Lord God. But that temple had been destroyed in 587 B.C. by the invading Babylonians. So the Jews now set about constructing a second temple. Herod began building a third temple in 20 B.C. Jews both in Palestine and throughout the Mediterranean world believed that God was present in the sacred place called the holy of holies. Throughout Judaism, Jerusalem and the temple were sacred. Jews went in pilgrimage to Jerusalem for the major feasts of Passover and Tabernacles. When Jews outside Palestine gathered in their local synagogues each Sabbath, they faced the temple in Jerusalem, so as to remember that they also shared in its daily sacrifices and major festivals. Now, in A.D. 70, the Romans had destroyed both city and temple; priests could no longer offer sacrifices to their God. As the Jewish people plunged into discouragement, they began to ask uncertainly how God would continue to be present to them.

During the Jewish revolt in Palestine, Nero, the reigning Roman emperor, blamed Christians for the fire in Rome and put many Christians to death, including Peter and Paul (A.D. 67–69). After Nero committed suicide, Rome experienced a year of political chaos (A.D. 68). Three emperors—Galba, Otho, and Vitellius—died by suicide or assassination. Revolts and unrest broke out not only in Palestine but also in Germany, Gaul, Africa, Britain, and Pontus. Roman authorities recalled Vespasian from leading the Roman army against the Jews in Palestine and crowned him emperor. His task was to restore order to the widespread Roman empire.

Nero's persecution, which shocked the Christians in Rome and the rest of the Christian world, had a strong impact on Christians in cities throughout the empire. The persecution deprived the Christian movement of its great missionary leaders—Peter and Paul. Moreover, Christians throughout the empire began to fear that Roman persecution might also extend to urban centers like Antioch.

Around A.D. 70 one of Peter's followers, probably to be identified as John Mark (Acts 12:12; 1 Pet 5:13), wrote the first gospel. He based his story about Jesus on Peter's preaching, as well as on oral and written traditions. Mark edited the data available to him to create a continuous story about Jesus of Nazareth which met the religious needs of his fellow Christians in Rome. Without the presence of Peter and Paul, these Christians now depended on stories to preserve their individual and collective memories of Jesus. Mark shaped the traditions about Jesus into his gospel around the end of the Jewish revolt (A.D. 70). He did this to support his Christian community as the city of Rome was preparing to welcome its triumphant armies back from Palestine with their booty from the temple in Jerusalem.

After A.D. 70, Jews in Palestine faced the enormous task of reconstructing Judaism after the devastating revolt against Rome. During the revolt, Johannan ben Zakkai, a leader among the Pharisees, received permission from Vespasian to establish a Jewish center at Jamnia, a city west of Jerusalem on the Mediterranean Sea. With other Pharisees, he formed a council that would later replace in influence the Jewish Sanhedrin in Jerusalem.

Defeat forced Jews in Palestine to live under still greater economic and political pressure. Rome gave land to those Jews whose political and religious sympathies they could trust, while they imposed heavier taxes on the common people. The revolt also left a vacuum of leadership within Judaism. Since Jerusalem and the temple were burned, the Sadducees lost their role as leaders. Few Essenes survived, since the Romans also destroyed their community in Qumran. Some Zealots fled to Masada where they held out against the Romans until A.D. 73. When Rome stormed that high rock fortress, the Zealots killed their families and each other rather than surrender to their enemies.

Under Johannan ben Zakkai, the Pharisees at Jamnia began to reconstruct Judaism. They controlled the Jewish calendar and with it the Jewish religion, since without worship in the temple their religion must now be based exclusively on observing the Jewish law. Johannan also regulated the conduct of priests, transferred parts of the temple ritual to local synagogues, and made rules about the gifts and offerings that Jews had given to support the temple. Traditional conflicts among the Pharisees were gradually settled in favor of Johannan and his fellow Hillelites. In Jamnia, Pharisees interpreted the Jewish law in ways that helped Jews maintain their religious identity despite the loss of the temple in Jerusalem.

The Pharisees also introduced an orderly codification of what had been their chaotic traditions of oral interpretation. Sages wrote down those oral traditions. Thus began a process that would lead to the formation of the Jewish Mishnah and ultimately to the Babylonian and Palestinian Talmuds as the official code of interpretation for Judaism. Scholars at Jamnia also tried to unify Judaism by tightly regulating the rules, rites, and customs of Jewish synagogues. To keep popular piety alive, they introduced into the synagogues rituals that would recall to their fellow Jews those previously practiced in the temple. Gradually the Pharisees also standardized worship in synagogues, established an official list of the Hebrew scriptures, and instituted their rabbinate as the authoritative interpreters of the Jewish law.

The Pharisees at Jamnia also began to confront the Christian movement, since it had also survived the devastating effects of defeat in the revolt against Rome. Christians claimed Jesus Christ as the Messiah. Their success in winning over Jews and Gentiles to their convictions about Jesus threatened the Pharisees. So the Pharisees began to threaten the Christian-Jews by making them feel unwelcome in their Jewish synagogues. The Pharisees at Jamnia introduced liturgical and non-liturgical practices aimed at excluding Christian-Jews. A new prayer, the Birkath ha Minim, was really a curse against the Christians. This prayer isolated the Christians, so that the authorities could ban them from the synagogues.

Nero's persecution in Rome, the destruction of Jerusalem and the temple, and the rise of Pharisaism in Jamnia combined to seriously threaten the Christian community in Antioch. Growing pressure caused internal scandal and dissension. Christians betrayed one another, and hatred among Christians increased. False prophets and false messiahs claimed to be anointed by God to lead the community. Confusion, disorientation, and conflict divided those who followed Jesus as their risen Lord. As wickedness spread, their love for each other grew cold.

Christians in Antioch also questioned their relationship to post-war Jamnia Pharisaism and even their identity as a movement rooted in Judaism within the Roman empire. In these uncertain times, they asked, can we continue to think of ourselves as a movement within Judaism? What attitude should we have toward the Pharisees at Jamnia? Should we accept their interpretation of the law? What about the tension and hostility that our Jewish members are experiencing in their synagogues? What about the threat of Roman persecution? Should we continue to focus our missionary efforts on the Jews or turn more to the Gentiles? What does being a community of Christians mean in these unstable times?

When Simeon ben Eliezer returned to Antioch after visiting his family, he found his community without answers to these crucial questions about their identity and mission. They turned to traditions about Jesus, including the gospel of Mark from Rome. They thought and prayed together about Jesus of Nazareth and about what significant persons, like Peter and Paul, had said and done. In this process they hoped to find a vision that might guide them and give them a sense of direction in their very uncertain times.

Almost two thousand years stand between us and Simeon's community in Antioch. Vast differences in culture also separate us—in religion and politics, in individual and social customs, in commerce and trade, in every aspect of life. We can never forget these historical and cultural differences. But like us, Simeon and his community lived in times that were unsafe and unpredictable.

In uncertain times, whether Simeon's or ours, we feel alienated from the world in which we live. Hearing about turmoil and suffering, we may feel overwhelmed and powerless. We may be tempted to say: "What's happening is just too overpowering to think about. I have to block most of it out. If I don't think about it, it might go away. What can I do anyway?" We become unable or unwilling to let ourselves think about and feel the pain in our world. Since we do not know how to translate knowing and caring into concrete action, we prefer not to know or care. Our feelings are numbed, as we confront situations that seem without meaning or hope. Thus, in uncertain times, we may respond with apathy.

Compassion, the opposite of apathy, means that we go where others are hurting, enter into their place of pain, and share in their brokenness and fear, in their confusion and anguish. Because others are hurting, we are willing to hurt too. Like the food we eat and the air we breathe, compassion is as natural to us as it was to Simeon and his community. We are not cut off from the pain in the world, but integral to it, like cells in a larger body. When one part is traumatized, we sense the trauma in the sufferings of our fellow humans. For Simeon, the trauma was the painful threats from Rome and Jamnia Pharisaism; for us the upheaval arises from small and large systems that are no longer able to provide a secure social environment.

Uncertain times can also prompt Christians to ask important questions about our faith and our place in the world: How are we to live as Christians? What are we to do? How are we to think and feel? Where do we turn to find truth and meaning? How do truth and meaning find us? Who is Jesus Christ and the God he calls his Father? What does following Jesus Christ mean? How do we see God in relation to ourselves in our world? What values do we want to foster in ourselves and others? What desires does God want us to have so that we make right decisions and design concrete strategies for action that can create a better world for ourselves and our children? Such questions troubled Simeon and his community in Antioch. We also ask them today.

Traditionalists may respond: "Everything is fine! Don't change anything! Cut out what doesn't fit! Put new life into traditional patterns of behavior!" Moderates may advise: "Accommodate the past! Adjust to our new situation! Grow, but always in harmony with our past!" Radicals may urge: "Break cleanly with the past! Create new solutions to meet our new times! Transform our world!"

Confusion can move us, as it moved Simeon and his

community, to reflect on our roots—the persons and experiences from which we have come as individuals and families, as Christian communities, as nations in a world society. As we recall our heritage, we remember significant persons and relive the events that have shaped our identity. We try to recapture the vision and recover the values of those who founded our communities.

As we tap into our roots, we may feel more grounded, more secure, more energetic, more creative, more empowered. We may gain new perspectives from which to view our present times. As we free our imaginations from negative thoughts and feelings, we begin to see new possibilities for our world. With that vision we can choose the values and make the decisions that can move us to work to build a more certain world.

Reflection Questions

- Right *now* what surfaces in you when you hear the phrase *uncertain times?* What images, thoughts, feelings, experiences, and so on come to you?
- In the *past* where have you encountered the times as uncertain in your own life, in the lives of others, in the church, in your country, in the world situation?

Recall and describe one or several concrete experiences. What events made you question your actions—Are we doing the right thing?—or even your identity—Who are we?

Recall and name your thoughts and feelings around the events: "I remember thinking . . . I remember feeling . . ."

Recall and name how you and others responded. Were your responses the same or different? Did you agree or disagree? Name the pain involved. Were you tempted to apathy? What gave you compassion?

Recall and describe the concrete strategies you chose and the actions you took. Where did you turn? Whose help did you enlist? What did you do?

• Complete the following sentence with adjectives, images, drawings, paintings, clay figures, or anything else: "At this moment my relationship to 'uncertain times' is best described as ＿＿＿＿＿ ."

Readings

For a thorough study of the historical background see S. Freyne, *The World of the New Testament.* Wilmington: Michael Glazier, 1980. R.E. Brown and J.P. Meier, *Antioch and Rome.* Mahwah: Paulist Press, 1983.

For a discussion of our times see J.R. Macy, *Despair and Personal Power in the Nuclear Age.* Baltimore: New Society, 1983. P.R. Loeb, *Hope in Hard Times.* Lexington: D.C. Heath, 1987.

2

Reading Matthew's Story

Matthew's gospel is a story, a narrative, a tale. It is a tale about John the Baptist and Jesus, about Jesus and his Jewish followers, about Jewish and Gentile suppliants, about the crowds in Galilee and Jerusalem, about the enemies of Jesus, and about the Jewish and Roman authorities. The story includes five scenes in which Jesus teaches his followers what living in light of the kingdom means. Seldom do we read or hear the entire narrative as a story. In church we listen to a single event or a few sayings from the Sermon on the Mount or the parable discourse. Or we may read sections of the story in private. But to understand the vision of Matthew's gospel, we need to read it as a story about Jesus.

Because Matthew's story announces God's reign, God's powerful, faithful love for the world, we call it a gospel, a proclamation of good news. This gospel proclaims that the reign of God or, as Matthew calls it, the reign of heaven is present and active in the world through the words and actions of Jesus of Nazareth. Jesus preaches the good news, teaches in synagogues, heals every disease, tells stories called parables, debates with his enemies, suffers and dies, but rises to new life. He will come again. His words and actions disclose how God's power worked in the world during Jesus' earthly life, how God's power continues to work through the followers of Jesus in his risen life, and how God's power will finally be revealed when Jesus returns at the end of the age.

Matthew wrote this story so that his community in Antioch might believe more deeply in Jesus as Messiah and risen Lord and thereby be enabled to respond to their uncertain times. As they celebrated the eucharist, Jewish and Gentile Christians gathered in their homes to find the truth of the gospel and to reflect on its meaning.

Matthew's story has been read and reread in similar settings over the two thousand years that separate us from his community in Antioch. Christians have pondered it in different situations, in good times and in bad times. But Matthew's gospel has always remained a story about how Jesus Christ revealed the reign of God.

We receive this good news as a story, not as a letter or an essay, nor as a catechism of doctrinal statements. A mother receives each of her children as a unique and individual child. A shortstop sets himself differently to field a ground ball, a pop fly, or a line drive. We know how differently we read the telephone book, a letter from a close friend, a bank statement, or a novel. We approach these written texts with different expectations. What makes Matthew's gospel a story, a tale, a narrative? If we know this, we may be able to read his gospel with fresh eyes.

Like other narratives, Matthew's story has a plot. Plot is the arrangement of events—words and actions—into a continuous story. Matthew's plot represents an action that is whole and complete and of a certain length, breadth, and size. The action is *whole* because it has a beginning, a middle and an end. The action is *complete* because it comes to a conclusion. The action is *of a certain length, breadth, and size* because it extends over time and deals with significant events. In the plot of Matthew's story, events result from what has taken place before and are the natural outcome of what has preceded. Matthew arranged the events to call forth faith, trust, hope, and love in his readers.

How did Matthew organize the events in his story? Each event has its own setting, its own action, and its own response. How did the evangelist weave these events into a plot that invites his readers to have hope in uncertain times? To answer this question we will look at the dramatic movement of the story: the time and place, the cast of characters, the scenes in which the movement changes direction, and the scenes in which Jesus gives five distinctive discourses. We will conclude with a summary of the plot and with a process for reading the story.

a. Time and Place

Storytellers carefully tell their readers about the time and place of their story. Thus, we can follow the plot with a clock, a calendar, and a map. Matthew is far less careful about these movements of time and place. In the infancy narrative (Mt 1–2) we may find that following Joseph and Mary with their child from Bethlehem in Judea to Egypt and from Egypt back to Nazareth in Galilee is easy. But we do not know how long they sojourned in Egypt nor how old the child was when they returned to Nazareth.

Matthew then leaps over Jesus' childhood and adolescence to his public ministry (Mt 3–28). He tells us nothing about the years between the return from Egypt and the beginning of John's ministry at the Jordan. Within the public ministry, the broad movement from place to place is clear: John and Jesus in the desert in Judea (3:1–4:11); Jesus' ministry in Galilee (4:12–16:12); the journey to Jerusalem (16:13–20:34); events in Jerusalem (21:1–28:15); the appearance back in Galilee (28:16–20). But we simply do not know whether these events took six months, a year, or several years.

We may or may not be able to follow the movement from one event to the next. For example, we can track both time and place between the last supper, Jesus' prayer in the garden, his arrest and trial before the Jews, his trial before Pilate, his death on Calvary and his burial, the women's visit to the empty tomb, and the appearance to his disciples in Galilee (Mt 26–28). However, the scenes that disclose various reactions for or against Jesus (Mt 11–12) are not so clear as to time and place.

Matthew's story, however, has another time and place —that of the world revealed in the events. That world begins with the conception of Jesus the Christ and ends with his appearance as risen Lord. But it also extends back to Abraham and forward to Jesus' final coming at the close of the age. The first scene in Matthew's story presents a genealogy that begins with Abraham (1:1–17). Explicit citations of the Hebrew scriptures, as well as implicit echoes, especially in the early chapters, constantly remind us that this story about Jesus must be read in light of the story of Israel. In the final scene, Jesus promises his disciples that he will be with them until the end of the age, that is, until he returns as Son of Man on the clouds of heaven (28:16–20).

When we read Matthew's story, then, we may find that tracing the precise movement in time and place is more difficult with Matthew than with the modern novels of James Michener. The evangelist does not always tell us where each event takes place or how much time passes between events. As we read, we can keep an eye on the overall movement, but we should not expect to keep track of it from event to event. We should not be surprised if we get lost.

b. Cast of Characters

The principal character in the infancy narrative (Mt 1–2) is Joseph. Matthew traces Joseph's lineage from Abraham. Receiving messages from God in dreams, Joseph does what God commands. The magi are also important characters. They travel to Palestine, visit Herod in Jerusalem, pay homage to Jesus in Bethlehem, and return secretly to the east. Because Herod tries to trick the magi and commands that the children in Bethlehem be slaughtered, he is clearly an enemy of Jesus. At the center of the events stand Mary and the child, neither of whom acts or speaks.

Characters in the story of Jesus' public ministry (Mt 3–28) can be summarized in the accompanying diagram:

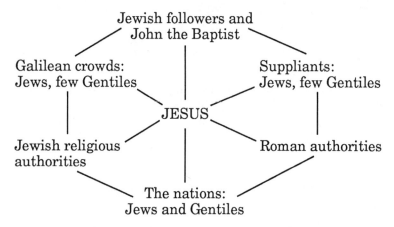

These characters may be round, flat, or stock. Since they are complex and unpredictable, *round* characters most resemble real people. We cannot predict their behavior, because they possess a variety of traits, some of which may even conflict. Jesus and his followers are round characters. *Flat* characters, who possess fewer traits, are generally more predictable in their behavior. For instance, the crowds always show wonder, enthusiasm, and amazement; the Jewish religious authorities are always hostile to Jesus. *Stock* characters have only one trait and fulfill a single role in the story. Thus, John the Baptist acts as a foil for Jesus, and Pilate becomes a foil for the Jewish religious authorities. Suppliants model faith in Jesus, as does the Roman centurion at the cross.

As the central character, Jesus is always doing or saying something in the story. His foil is John the Baptist, whose ministry, imprisonment, and cruel death anticipate that of Jesus. Jesus relates positively to three groups of characters: the followers, the suppliants, and the crowds. These groups model different responses to the words and actions of Jesus.

Followers walk behind Jesus. He teaches them, shares his work with them, explains his parables to them, and invites them to take on his view of suffering and death and to live according to his paradoxical values. Often curious, the followers ask Jesus questions. Jesus is their teacher, and they are his student-disciples, even though they often fail to understand his words. They leave home and occupation to follow Jesus, even though they vacillate in living out that radical commitment.

Suppliants are the men and women, mostly Jews but a few Gentiles, who model faith by asking to be cured: the leper and the paralytic, Jairus and the woman with a hemorrhage. Jesus often tells them, "Your faith has made you whole." What does he mean by faith? He means that these persons know they are in need, are convinced that Jesus can do something to meet their need, and act out their conviction in word or action. Once cured, they disappear from the story. Matthew does not tell us that they joined the followers committed to Jesus.

Crowds in Galilee react positively to Jesus' words and

actions and follow him to Jerusalem. Predominantly Jewish, they act like a chorus in an opera or a play. They watch what Jesus does and listen to his words. They respond with wonder, amazement, and enthusiasm. Matthew records them as saying, "We have never seen anything like this . . . He speaks with authority . . . Could this be the Messiah?" These interested spectators do not commit themselves to follow Jesus, and in the end they side with his enemies in asking for his death.

Jewish religious authorities are Jesus' enemies. They include the scribes and Pharisees, the Sadducees, the chief priests and elders of the people. From the ministry of John (3:7–12), Matthew presents them as hostile to the reign of God revealed in Jesus. Matthew does not tell us how they became hostile, nor does he show that they are given a chance to repent. When they attempt to trick Jesus, he wins every debate. Jesus warns his followers and the crowds about these authorities. As Jesus' enemies, they represent the evil forces that oppose God's power at work in Jesus' words and actions. Distinguishing these authorities from the predominantly Jewish crowds is important.

Roman authorities are Pilate, the Roman procurator, and his soldiers who put Jesus to death on the cross. Included in this group is the centurion who in witnessing the events of Jesus' death believes that he is the Son of God. The *nations* are the Jews and Gentiles to whom the risen Jesus sends his followers. These people will be judged at the end of the age according to how they welcomed the disciples.

As we read, we may want to follow these characters through the story. Which characters change? Which remain the same? How does the network develop and grow? Which characters are more central? How do they relate to each other in each block of events? Tracing the characters may prove easier than following the movement in time and place.

c. Scenes in Which the Movement Changes Direction

The movement of the plot pivots on hinge-events. Doors swing open and close on their hinges. So the movement in Matthew's story swings on certain events. Other metaphors provide us with insights on these events: streams of water gather into reservoirs, rest there for a moment, and then pour out in new directions. Like reservoirs, these hinge-events echo what went before (the stream) and announce what is to come (the new direction). As certain patterns in a tapestry collect different threads together, so these events gather the threads of the narrative. As certain moments in a symphony recapitulate earlier themes and introduce new themes, so these events recapitulate and announce the themes in Matthew's story. They attract our attention precisely because they introduce a new movement in the plot.

A hinge-event (1) advances the plot, (2) echoes what goes before and announces what follows, (3) occasions a puzzling or difficult problem (crux) in the narrative, (4) cannot be deleted without destroying the logic of the plot, (5) calls for completion by another hinge-event, and so (6) forms a sequence of events that serves as an outline of the plot.

Matthew's story begins with the conception and birth of Jesus the Christ (1:1–25). This beginning, which is the foundation for all that follows, fulfills God's promises to Abraham, continues the line of David, and completes the return from exile. Reading this as story, we wonder how the episodes that follow will be related to these key persons and events in Israel's history.

The ministry of John the Baptist at the Jordan is the next pivotal event (3:1–12). A leap in time! A new beginning! John the Baptist appears at the Jordan. He preaches the reign of God, invites the people to a baptism of repentence, warns the Sadducees and Pharisees, and speaks about his relationship to the Messiah. We wonder who that Messiah will be and how he will relate to John.

The next hinge in the story is the beginning of Jesus' public ministry in Galilee (4:12–25). John's arrest signals the beginning. Leaving Nazareth, Jesus centers his activities in Capernaum. He calls four fishermen, and they follow him. Throughout Galilee, he preaches the gospel of the kingdom, teaches in the Jewish synagogues, and heals every disease and every infirmity among the people. Crowds from the four corners of Palestine bring their sick to be healed. We wonder how the people in Galilee, both Jews and Gentiles, will respond.

Another pivotal event occurs when Jesus sends the twelve disciples on their mission (9:35–10:4). He shares with them his power to preach the kingdom and to heal every disease. He sends them not to the Gentiles but to the lost sheep of the house of Israel. We wonder why Jesus excludes the Samaritans and the Gentiles.

When John sends questions to Jesus and Jesus gives his answers (11:2–6), we encounter another hinge-event. John the Baptist, still in prison, sends messengers to inquire if Jesus is the Messiah; thus he raises the question that Israel must answer. On the basis of Jesus' preaching, teaching, and healing do they recognize him as their Messiah? We pause to wonder how the characters are reacting to Jesus at this point in the story.

New movement is introduced when Herod refers to John the Baptist raised from the dead (14:1–12). Matthew then flashes back to describe how Herod had John the Baptist beheaded. Since John has already been a foil for Jesus, we wonder whether a similar death awaits Jesus at the hands of his enemies.

Conversations at Caesarea Philippi mark the next hinge-event (16:13–28). Caesarea Philippi is the first stop on the journey to Jerusalem. Jesus asks his disciples what people have been saying about him. Then he inquires what the disciples themselves have to say about him on the basis of what they have seen and heard. Peter responds with titles for Jesus, and Jesus responds with titles for Peter. However, when Jesus announces that he must suffer, die, and be raised, Peter rebukes him. Jesus in turn admonishes Peter. Jesus then instructs his disciples. Experiencing tension, we wonder whether Jesus' predictions will come true, whether his followers will ever understand, and what taking up his cross and following him means.

When Jesus enters Jerusalem and takes possession of the temple (21:1–17), the plot takes another step forward. These events cause Jesus' enemies, especially the Pharisees, to plot his death. We wonder what his fate will be in Jerusalem, what will happen to the blind men and the others who follow him into the city, and whether the Jewish authorities will ever recognize Jesus as their Messiah.

The next hinge discloses the plotting of Jesus' death and the resurrection (26:1–16). As the Pharisees determine to kill Jesus, a woman at Bethany anoints his body for burial. We wonder whether Jesus will escape their plot or actually suffer, die, and be raised, as he has predicted. We wonder if the story will end with his hurried burial.

The great commission brings us to the last event and the climax of the story (28:16–20). Back in Galilee, Jesus returns to his followers as their risen Lord and sends them out on mission to all nations, to both Jews and Gentiles. Matthew ends his story with a new beginning that leaves us wondering how the mission will be carried out, what will happen to those who are sent, and what will be the final outcome at the end of the age.

d. Five Distinctive Discourses

In reading Matthew's story we are struck by the five scenes in which Jesus teaches his disciples and the crowds. Sometimes he teaches both the disciples and the crowds; sometimes he instructs only the disciples. These five collections of Jesus' sayings are the sermon on the mount (5:1–7:28), the mission discourse (10:1–42), the parable discourse (13:1–53), the community discourse (17:22–18:35), and the eschatological discourse (24:1–25:46).

In the sermon on the mount (5:1–7:28) Jesus presents his platform. He teaches what living in the reign of God means. He sketches its vision of life, its values, and its attitudes. In the mission discourse (10:1–42) Jesus tells the twelve disciples how they are to carry out their mission to the lost sheep of the house of Israel, what they can expect, and how Israel will be judged. In the parable discourse (13:1–53) Jesus tells his disciples and the crowds simple stories that reveal the secrets of God's reign, but only to his disciples does he explain the meaning hidden in the stories.

In the community discourse (17:22–18:35) Jesus teaches his disciples how to live together in community. They must avoid scandal, go after the one sheep gone astray, reconcile the member who has sinned, and forgive one another without limit. In the eschatological discourse (24:1–25:46) Jesus envisions the future. He tells his disciples about the tribulations that they can expect, but he also promises that he will return at the end of the age to judge both them and all the nations.

Summary of the Plot

When we put together the movement in time and place, the cast of characters, the scenes in which the plot changes direction, and the five discourses, we come up with the following summary of the plot in Matthew's story:

- Infancy Narrative: Story in Miniature (1:1–2:23)
- John the Baptist and Jesus in the Judean Desert (3:1–4:11)
- Jesus Preaches, Teaches, and Heals in Galilee (4:12–9:34)
- Jesus and the Twelve Disciples: Mission to Israel (9:35–10:42)
- Israel Reacts; Jesus Teaches in Parables (11:1–13:58)
- Jesus Forms the Disciples; Events Concerning Bread (14:1–16:12)
- Journey to Jerusalem; Initiation into Paradox (16:13–20:34)
- Jesus and the Temple in Jerusalem; Predicting the End of the Age (21:1–25:46)
- Passover Meal, Passion, Death, and Resurrection (26:1–28:20)

How does Matthew want his original readers in Antioch to respond to his story? The end provides the answer. He wants them to imitate the disciples in worshiping their risen Lord, even as they continue to wonder and doubt. He also wants his community to have confidence derived from the sure knowledge that the promise to Abraham has been fulfilled in their risen Lord. Matthew assures his listeners that Jesus sends them and remains present to them as they preach their good news to the nations and that Jesus will return at the end of the age to complete his mission, establishing forever the reign of God over all the nations. In a word, Matthew wants his readers to have *hope,* that is, to continue choosing life even in their uncertain times.

Exercise

I have reflected on the gospel of Matthew as a story about Jesus from his conception to his resurrection. I have talked about its movement, its characters, its hinge-events, its discourses, and its overall movement. Now I invite you to read Matthew's entire story. If possible, do this in one sitting. Focus your attention on the individual words, phrases, and sentences. Become more aware of each element in the story.

When some time has elapsed after your first reading, you might want to read Matthew's story again from beginning to end. At this time focus more on its sense lines, units of thought, scenes in their sequence, characters in their interaction. Attend to the feel of the story: Does it feel hard or soft, warm or cold, close or far away, inviting or uninviting? Later still, you may want to read the story a third time. This time you will attend more to the feelings that surface in you as you grow more familiar with the story.

After each reading, you may want to do the following exercise:

1. Select three adjectives to complete each of the following sentences. For each adjective indicate a passage in Matthew's story that supports your choice.

- Matthew's gospel is ....
- Matthew's Jesus is ....
- The relationship between Matthew's Jesus and his followers is ....

- The relationship between Matthew's Jesus and the Jewish religious authorities is ....
- The relationship between Matthew's Jesus and the Jewish crowds is ....
- The relationship between Matthew's Jesus and the suppliants is ....

2. Think about your response to Matthew's story and answer these questions:

- What aspects of the story appeal to me the most?
- What do I find especially meaningful?
- What aspects did I ignore?
- What is my overall reaction to Matthew's story?

Readings

For further treatment of Matthew's gospel as a story see:

R.A. Edwards, *Matthew's Story of Jesus*. Philadelphia: Fortress Press, 1985. J.D. Kingsbury, *Matthew as Story*. Philadelphia: Fortress Press, 1986. F.J. Matera, "The Plot of Matthew's Gospel," *Catholic Biblical Quarterly* 49 (1987) 233–253.

3

Praying with Matthew's Story

Matthew's story about Jesus also provides us with an opportunity to deepen our relationship with God through prayer. A man of faith wrote this good news for a community that believed in Jesus as their risen Lord. Receiving the story today as persons who also believe in Jesus Christ, we may want to pray with it as a means to encounter both Jesus and the God whose reign he reveals. Through prayer we make ourselves available for that encounter, whether as individuals, small groups, or worshiping communities.

Our faith shapes our praying with Matthew's story. We believe that God wants to encounter us in prayer just as we want to encounter God and that we can encounter God in any place or at any time. However, Matthew's story, as God's inspired word, is a privileged place for that encounter. These convictions draw us to pray with Matthew.

Above all, we are convinced that prayer is a gift. In prayer we touch our deepest desire to know and love God, to be known and loved by God, to encounter God and be encountered by God in our lives. We recognize that this desire is a gift from God and that God is more eager to speak to us and communicate with us than we are open to listen or respond. God gives us the desire to pray and calls us to prayer. God invites us into relationship and enables

us to respond to that invitation. We do not achieve dialogue in prayer through our own efforts. All is gift—want-
ing to pray, accepting God's invitation to pray, and
answering freely. Therefore, a basic attitude in prayer is a
gratitude based on faith. This gratitude quiets us and
opens us to the reality of God in our lives.

Because Matthew's story about Jesus of Nazareth is
the inspired word of God, it can be a springboard for
prayer. This story invites us to be with Jesus, with the men
and women who follow him, with the suppliants and
crowds who come to him, and with the Pharisees and other
Jewish religious authorities who are his enemies. As we
hear the story, we also listen for the risen Jesus who may
want to meet us in his words and actions. We believe that
Matthew's gospel is simultaneously a document from the
past and the words of a living Lord who desires to speak to
us today. We need to take the time to listen to the story
with faith, to let it sink into deeper levels of our awareness.
When we attend to the story, the risen Jesus recreates and
nourishes us, supports and challenges us, and guides us
with his vision and values in these uncertain times.

As a springboard, Matthew's gospel readies us for a
loving encounter with Jesus. Because we want to be with
Jesus, we prepare for his coming as we prepare for a visit
with any other friend. We invite him into our lives by
setting aside a regular time to be together and by asking
him to speak to us and to teach us how to listen. Matthew's
story enables us to be there with Jesus and to be attentive
with our minds and with our hearts.

As we listen to the events in Matthew's story, we also
listen with faith for Jesus. We listen simply, deeply, and
reverently. We hunger to be nourished by his presence. We
are grateful for the faith that brings us to prayer. We refrain from searching the story for its hidden meanings,
implications, or applications. We resist drawing conclu-

sions or making resolutions. We let Jesus be with us. We allow Jesus to do whatever he wishes. We let him speak to us, heal and forgive us, confront and challenge us, console and strengthen us. We let him lead us into deserts and storms, into green meadows and calm seas. Entrusting ourselves to Jesus, we wait for him to encounter us in love.

We respond to Jesus in any way we feel moved to respond. We respond freely and spontaneously, genuinely and honestly, reverently and respectfully. We speak what is in our minds and hearts. We say whatever we think and feel, whether positive or negative. We ask or thank, adore or complain, praise or blame. When we do not know what to say, we communicate without words. We let the Holy Spirit pray in and for us in our weakness. Seeking to be transparent with the risen Jesus, we invite him to know and love us as the persons we know ourselves to be.

Praying with Matthew's story, then, means spending time with Jesus, with God the Father, and with the Holy Spirit. As we listen and respond, we do not strive to encounter God nor try to control the encounter. We trust that God seeks to encounter us. We simply spend time with God. We let God be for us the loving God revealed in the words and actions of Jesus. We know that God will make Jesus more alive and real to us in our everyday lives.

One method for praying with Matthew's story is called *simple reading.* The key to this method is simplicity. For five or ten minutes a day, we read Matthew's gospel the way we read any story. To begin we settle into a comfortable posture that is conducive to listening to God. For a few minutes we relax and quiet ourselves. Next, we give all our cares to the Lord, letting God hold them, while we spend this time in prayer. We may even take the phone off the hook, so that we can have this uninterrupted time with God.

Then we slowly read a section of Matthew's story like

"Jesus Preaches, Teaches, and Heals in Galilee" (4:12–9:34). Believing that the words are God's own words to us here and now, we let ourselves receive the story as good news. As we read, we may find one or more resting places in the narrative. We stop when we find ourselves drawn into the story or when we resist it. We linger, savor, repeat, and reflect in silence. We let the text open up, so that in listening to it we may also listen for the Lord.

We begin to respond by talking to Jesus from our concrete life-situation. We resist analyzing the story or applying it to our life. Instead, we let ourselves gradually discover similarities between events in the story and events in our own life—between Jesus inviting four fishermen to follow him and the same Lord calling us, between his teaching in the sermon on the mount and what we need to learn, between his healings and our need to be healed. As we become aware of resemblances between the two stories, we focus on listening and responding to the Lord out of our reactions. We attend to Matthew's story only as it serves our encounter with the Lord.

Another popular method for praying with Matthew's story is *sacred reading* ("lectio divina"). After preparing for prayer and recalling God's presence, we *read* about an event in Matthew's story, such as Jesus calming the storm at sea (8:23–27). Reading the passage slowly, we dwell on each word and phrase. We read several times, out loud if possible, until something in the text especially draws or repels us. At that point, we begin to *meditate,* that is, to think about what is alerting our mind and heart. We ask questions about what the event might mean: What is the action? Why is it going on? What is the physical setting? What is the time? Who are the persons in the event? Who does what, and why? Who speaks? What happens in response? With whom do we most identify? What is most central in the event?

As we think and reason, we may begin to sense similarities between the storm at sea and the storms in our lives. We may notice what Jesus reveals about himself both in the event and in our experience. We may even begin to move into conversation with Jesus in *prayer.* We speak spontaneously or remain silent in his presence. We close the scripture, shut our eyes, and open our hearts to this encounter with the Lord. We remain fixed in that moment of prayer as long as we are not distracted. When distractions make concentration in prayer difficult, we read Matthew's account of the event again and move again from reading to meditation and from meditation to deeper prayerful awareness. "Sacred reading," an excellent form of prayer for people who want to pray with both mind and heart, enables us not only to meditate with our minds but also to move from thinking to more heart-centered prayer.

At times we may prefer to pray with a method called *imaginative contemplation.* After quieting ourselves and preparing for prayer, we let our imaginations create the entire setting for Jesus' calming of the storm at sea. We let the scene present itself to us, and we present ourselves to the scene. Before the action starts, we construct the setting in our imaginations by asking questions such as the following: What kind of boat is Jesus in with his followers? Is the boat clean or dirty? How large or small is the lake? Is the water rough or calm? What is the weather like? Is the night clear or cloudy? Is the moon shining?

With the scene set, we let the whole event come alive. We see the persons—Jesus, the crowds, and his followers. We continue to image by asking questions like the following about the characters: How many people are in the boat? What sort of persons are they? How are they dressed? What are they saying and doing? Why?

Next, we place ourselves in the boat; we move *into* the story and take part in it. Now we observe ourselves and ask: What are we doing? Why have we come? How do we feel as we look around at the other persons? Do we speak to anyone? To whom? About what? How do they respond?

With ourselves in the event we notice the central characters: Who are they? Where are they? How are they dressed? Is anyone with them?

We walk up and speak to the central characters, and we let them respond. Our imaginations continue to question: What do we say to them? What do they reply? As we get comfortable with these characters, we try to find out who they are, what they do, why they are here. We notice the impression they make on us. We consider how we feel as we interact with them.

We begin to notice Jesus. We watch his actions and listen to his words. Our imaginations picture him as we ask: Where does he go? How does he act? What does he say? What is he thinking? How is he feeling?

Jesus now comes toward us and the others. Our imaginations continue to paint the picture. We ask ourselves: What do we feel as he approaches? How do we feel when he talks to someone else? What does he say to the person? How does the person respond? We listen to the dialogue and watch the actions. We notice how the others react, then how Jesus reacts, and especially how we react to what we are seeing and hearing.

Jesus now turns to us. What does he say or do? How do we respond? We talk to him about how this event relates to the storms in our lives. We spend time with him in prayer, with or without words. This encounter with the risen Lord has been the gift we have desired: "To see thee more clearly, love thee more dearly, follow thee more nearly day by day."

Imaginative contemplation may appeal to persons who find that imagining the events of Matthew's story is easy. Sacred reading, however, may appeal more to those who prefer to think about and reflect on the same events. Because of our temperament, our personal preferences, or our concrete situation, we may be drawn to one method rather than to another. But we must always remember that the methods are only the means of encountering Jesus in love.

A good method for praying with Jesus' sayings can be called *prayer without words.* For example, we may be drawn to what Jesus says to his followers in the boat: "Why are you afraid, O men of little faith?" Again we recall God's presence and prepare ourselves for prayer. We then say Jesus' words to ourselves silently or out loud. Whichever way we choose, we simply repeat the words without trying to analyze or understand them. To receive these words into our hearts, repetition is essential. Then the words become part of our inner world.

As we savor these few words, they may begin to fit our experience, they may blend with our life. Or one word or phrase may speak to us. After some time we may feel deeply nourished by the words. We may want to speak spontaneously to Jesus, or we may feel drawn to a loving silence in his presence. Since we seek the Lord in prayer, we want to be as fully attentive as we can.

Scripture sharing is a method for group prayer with Matthew's story. After the group has recalled God's presence and prepared for prayer, the members read aloud the scriptural passage. (Because the group reads together, each person needs a copy of the same translation of the text.) Next, the leader invites the members to reflect quietly on a question related to this event, such as, "When was the last time you felt as though you were in a storm at sea?" After personal reflection, the participants share with each other as much of their reflections as they wish.

Next, the members read the text aloud together again. The leader then invites them to reflect privately on the following questions: "Where were you drawn into the passage? Where did you resist?" After time for personal reflection, the leader invites individuals to share as much as they wish to share. Lastly, the leader encourages the members to use the text as a springboard to pray together in silence or with words. The group then spends time in prayer and ends with an Our Father.

Praying with Matthew's story is much more to be experienced than described. Prayer, as we have noted before, is a pure gift, which is given when, how, and to the extent the Lord wishes to grant it. Only with patience can we know and believe in prayer, hope for and desire it, wait for and accept it. We come to prayer convinced that the Jesus we meet in the story is not dead but alive, not a fallen hero of the distant past but our risen Lord who reveals himself to us in and through the events in Matthew's story.

As we let Matthew share Jesus with us, we relive the events of his earthly life as the Christian Jews and Gentiles in Antioch relived them. Matthew wrote his story to help those followers of Jesus face their hopes and fears, their dreams and nightmares, their faith and doubt. Desiring to be drawn to a deeper faith in the risen Lord and to a stronger commitment to follow him in our uncertain times, we also pray with Matthew's story. Letting Jesus into our everyday lives, we invite him to share his life with us. In the mysterious encounter that is prayer, Jesus becomes more real and alive to us, his Father more our God and Father, and their Spirit more the Spirit that transforms our lives.

However, we cannot predict or control either the experience or the outcome of praying with Matthew's story of Jesus. At times we feel strongly and deeply connected to the Lord. Then we want to say, "Lord, I believe . . . Lord, it is good to know you . . . I trust you . . . Teach me to trust you more . . . Lord, you really do love me, and I really love you . . . Thank you, Lord."

At other times we feel a deep sense of inner peace, even though our lives remain as chaotic as a storm at sea. Although hectic activities complicate our lives, we have a sense that we are not alone, that Jesus travels with us through all the daily challenges. Because we know that we are in good relationship with God, we move into and through our days with peace. Thankful for that awareness, we look for God in the daily events of our lives.

At still other times, however, we get nothing from our prayer. We find Matthew's story boring, and the time we spend in prayer feels like eternity. Since prayer has lost all attraction and seems a total waste of time, we feel discouraged and tempted to stop praying. At such times we need to recall that we do not come to prayer so that something will happen. No. Prayer is our time to be with the risen Lord. Sometimes Jesus chooses to sit with us in silence. But the silence can be fruitful in days to come. We need to remind ourselves that our relationship with Jesus grows stronger as we remain faithful to reserving uninterrupted time for prayer, faithful even when we do not feel like praying. We must not gauge our success in prayer by how we feel during the time of prayer. Instead, we need to accept that our prayer expresses our desire to know the risen Lord and to let him be with us on our life's journey. Even though our prayer did not yield a good feeling, we are comforted with the realization that we have spent time sitting at the feet of the risen Lord.

Praying with Matthew's story may also awaken in us the desire to study this gospel more carefully because studying Matthew's story can enrich our prayer. As we pray, we may begin to wonder about Matthew's portrait of Jesus and the disciples, about the dramatic movement of his story, and about its vision of what being Christians in the world means. We may even want to study Matthew's story apart from our prayer. Studying the story enriches our prayer; praying with it stimulates further study. This dynamic interaction between prayer and study deepens our appreciation of Matthew's story, of our faith in the risen Lord whom the story reveals, and of our understanding of what following the Lord in uncertain times means.

Reflection Questions

- What surfaces in you when you hear the words *prayer* and *praying with Matthew's story?*
- When do you pray? How do you pray? Do you prefer to pray alone or in a group?
- Have you ever prayed with a gospel? In what way was this a positive or a negative experience?

Readings

For further thoughts on and methods for praying with scripture, see: W.G. Thompson, "Praying with Mark," "Praying with John," in *The Gospels for Your Whole Life.* San Francisco: Winston Press/Harper and Row, 1983, pp. 15–35, 99–111. Also, "Praying with Paul's Letters," in *Paul and His Message For Life's Journey.* Mahwah: Paulist Press, 1986, pp. 109–137. R. McDonnell, *Prayer Pilgrimage Through Scripture.* Mahwah: Paulist Press, 1984. Also, *Prayer Pilgrimage with Paul.* Mahwah: Paulist Press, 1985. M. Gallagher, C. Wagner, D. Woeste, *Praying with Scripture.* Mahwah: Paulist Press, 1983.

For a good overview of prayer, see: T. Greene, *Opening to God.* Notre Dame: Ave Maria Press, 1977. Also, *When the Well Runs Dry.* Notre Dame: Ave Maria Press, 1979. Also, *Darkness in the Market Place.* Notre Dame: Ave Maria Press, 1981. Also, *Wheat Among the Weeds.* Notre

Dame: Ave Maria Press, 1984. J.E. Schmidt, *Praying Our Experiences.* Winona: St. Mary's Press, 1980.

For a more thorough treatment see: L. Boase, *The Prayer of Faith.* Chicago: Loyola University Press, 1985. D.J. Hassel, *Radical Prayer.* Mahwah: Paulist Press, 1984. Also, *Dark Intimacy.* Mahwah: Paulist Press, 1986. J. Laplace, *Prayer According to the Scriptures,* and *Prayer: Desire and Encounter.* Brighton: Religious of the Cenacle. M.B. Pennington, *Centering Prayer.* Garden City: Doubleday, 1980.

4

Meeting Matthew
the Evangelist

Who was Matthew the evangelist? Why did he create a new story of Jesus? How did he create it? What sources did he use? When did he finish the final version? What was the role of the Holy Spirit? How does Matthew suggest that we receive his story? After reading the story and perhaps beginning to use it for prayer, we will want to spend some time in an imaginary conversation with the evangelist. We will question him, listen to his answers and further explain the process by which his story was created.

To begin our interview, we ask: "Who are you, Matthew? How would you describe yourself?"

Matthew responds: "In my story you meet a tax collector named 'Matthew.' When Jesus calls him, that tax collector leaves his occupation to follow Jesus (9:9). Later Jesus names Matthew as one of his twelve closest companions (10:3). I am not that Matthew. I am a third generation Jew-become-Christian. The community in Antioch to which I belong claims that original Matthew as its link to the historical Jesus. His authority stands behind my story. I never saw or heard Jesus during his life on earth. I came to know him through the traditions that go back to that converted tax collector and to his companions. Ever since Jesus' death and resurrection we have told and retold

stories about what he did and said. Some years ago we
began to write down some of these stories. We wanted to be
sure they wouldn't be lost. My community asked me to edit
those traditional stories about Jesus. So I've selected those
that speak most directly to our needs, and I've woven them
together into a new story about Jesus. That's the gospel,
the good news, you have read."

Our study of Matthew's story with its orderly plot tells
us that its editor/author must have been well educated.
Knowing Greek well, he was at home with the literary
forms and methods of his time. He had a thorough knowledge of the Hebrew scriptures, as well as of the methods
used by Jews to interpret those scriptures. His story reflects the concern he must have had for order, balance, and
structure.

The evangelist may also have identified himself with
the scribe whom Jesus named when he said, "Therefore
every scribe who has been trained for the kingdom of
heaven is like a householder who brings out of his treasure
what is new and what is old" (13:52). Like those who
shaped the traditions he used, the evangelist respected his
Jewish heritage and wanted to remain in touch with his
roots. But his dedication to Jesus as the risen Lord led him
to reinterpret that heritage in response to the uncertain
times that his community faced in post-war Judaism.

Like a householder with an attic full of family treasures, the evangelist brought elements of his Jewish tradition into conversation with his community's experience of
post-war Judaism and antagonism with Rome. His new
story about Jesus emerged from that dialogue. An insightful interpreter of Jesus, he showed how new things and old
can be found in the treasured stories of Jesus' words and
actions, and how they could shape the Christian community in Antioch.

We continue to question the evangelist by asking,

"Why did you create a new story of Jesus? How did you create it? What sources did you use? Where and when did you finish the final version?"

Matthew answers: "As you may know, our times were uncertain. We lived in a time that differed from the time in which Mark wrote his gospel. Mark wrote for Christians in Rome immediately after Nero's persecution and the Jewish revolt in Palestine (A.D. 70). In our formal worship and informal conversations in Antioch, we read and reflected upon Mark's story. As we experienced increasing tension with the Pharisees, we adapted Mark's story to fit our new situation. When we were expelled from our Jewish synagogues, we needed to incorporate Mark's gospel into a new story about Jesus that would speak more directly to our changed situation.

"I am well educated in our Jewish heritage and skilled in writing. So the community asked me to edit the earlier traditions about Jesus. I reworked Mark's gospel, a collection of sayings attributed to Jesus, and several other stories and sayings that we had received from earlier generations. Since we cherished those traditions, I tried to remain as faithful to them as I could, as I adapted them to our needs. I created my own plot for the first thirteen chapters of the story by weaving events from Mark and from my other sources into a new and more ordered account of the first days of Jesus' public ministry. For the rest of my story I added material to Mark's original plot.

"I completed the new story about Jesus around A.D. 85, that is, about fifteen years after the Jewish revolt in Palestine (A.D. 66–70) and after Nero's persecution in Rome (A.D. 67–69). I created the gospel for my still predominantly Jewish-Christian community in Syrian Antioch. At that time we were struggling with post-war developments within Judaism and with the threat of Roman persecution."

Matthew's story is not a biography of Jesus, like biographies of Abraham Lincoln or Martin Luther King, Jr. We expect modern biographers to give us an accurate description of what their subjects said and did during their lives. However, we cannot expect this of Matthew. His story is certainly rooted in the events of Jesus' earthly life and clearly reflects the man who walked the roads of Palestine in the early decades of the first century. Matthew's story portrays Jesus' words and actions in a way that we can trust. However, Matthew's gospel is a portrait of Jesus, not a photograph. It is rooted in the men and women who followed Jesus, saw what he did, heard what he said, and watched him interact with his enemies and with the crowds attracted to him. But it is more than an exact account because these eyewitnesses were entrusted with Jesus' memory and his message. By telling stories they transmitted their memories and his message to the first communities of Christians.

During the more than fifty years between Jesus' death and Matthew's story, Christian communities dedicated themselves to living and proclaiming the traditions about Jesus. Convinced that he was their risen Lord, they engaged in a vigorous mission to carry his message to Jews and Gentiles throughout the Hellenistic world. Their success convinced them that Jesus' victory over death had introduced a new era of God's salvation. So they worked all the harder to proclaim that good news in Palestine, as well as in Egypt and Syria, in Asia Minor and Greece, and even in Rome, the capital of the empire.

New Christian communities came to know Jesus through stories about what he did and collections of what he said. As they repeated the stories and sayings, these believers reflected on what these treasured words might mean for them and how the stories and sayings might shape their lives as individuals and as communities. They interpreted Jesus' words and actions in the light of both the Hebrew scriptures and the religious documents from the Hellenistic world. The stories they retold spoke to the problems they faced and to the concrete decisions they needed to make. They put together stories about Jesus' miracles or conflicts with his enemies; they also collected his sayings. They retold the events of his passion, death, and resurrection as one continuous narrative. While these communities knew the general outline of Jesus' ministry in Galilee and his death and resurrection in Jerusalem, they did not weave the traditions about Jesus into one coherent story.

Traditions about Jesus shaped the first Christian communities, and in turn their experience reshaped those traditions. As they recalled Jesus' miracles and conflicts, they omitted unnecessary details. Thus they highlighted how Jesus won every contest with disease or with his enemies. They modified or amplified Jesus' words, and they even put words on his lips that might respond to their needs. They combed the Hebrew scriptures to find the deeper meaning of Jesus' death and resurrection and retold that story to show how those events were part of God's plan for the world.

With the death of Peter and Paul in Nero's persecution, the Holy Spirit inspired the Christian community in Rome to write a continuous story of Jesus. Entrusted with that task was Mark, one of Peter's closest disciples. Mark created the first gospel around A.D. 70. Fifteen years later, around A.D. 85, Matthew the evangelist combined Mark's gospel with other traditions to provide his community in Antioch with a new story about Jesus. At the same time and perhaps in the same place, Luke the evangelist created an epic story about both Jesus and the earliest days of the

Christian movement. We read Luke's epic today, as Luke-Acts.

Matthew's story, his good news for uncertain times, is the product of a complicated process within the life of the Christian movement, as it moved out to Jews and Gentiles throughout the Roman empire. Matthew's gospel is not a family album with old photographs lovingly glued on each page. Instead it is a story about Jesus that is rooted in the events of his earthly life, as those events have been interpreted in the living tradition of the Christian movement.

Matthew wrote his story in Greek. His Greek is better than Mark's, but not as elegant as Luke's. Matthew frequently clarified Mark's vocabulary and improved his style. His story has a much stronger Jewish flavor than Mark's because his community in Antioch was more attuned to Jewish ways of using symbolic numbers and was more familiar with the Hebrew scriptures than was Mark's community in Rome. Matthew refers to the geography of Palestine more accurately than Mark. Matthew also omits Mark's explanations of Jewish customs because his community did not need the explanations.

Revealing his Jewish background, Matthew often arranges his material in numerical groups of three: three temptations (4:1–11), three sets of three miracles (8:1–9:34), three scenes of judgment (25:1–46). He also favors seven: seven parables about the reign of God (13:1–53), seven woes against the scribes and Pharisees (23:13–36), seven parables about the second coming (24:37–25:46).

Matthew interprets and explains Jesus' words and actions against the background of the Hebrew scriptures. He often includes direct quotations, especially in the events of the infancy narrative. This can be seen in the naming of Jesus (1:22–23), the visit of the magi (2:5–6), the flight into

Egypt (2:15), the massacre of the innocents (2:17–18), and the return to Nazareth (2:23). Less obvious allusions to the Hebrew scriptures inform events such as the temptations in the desert (4:1–11) and the death of Jesus (27:32–54). Matthew also associates Jesus with Abraham, Moses, and David. Both the Jewish and the Gentile members of Matthew's community in Antioch must have been well acquainted with the Hebrew scriptures.

Because Matthew uses several literary techniques to help his readers remember the story, his gospel is more ordered than Mark's. We have already seen how he uses echoes and foreshadowings in hinge-passages that disclose the movement of the plot. Summaries sometimes serve as refrains to keep readers in touch with the plot (4:23; 9:35; 11:1). Each of the five discourses ends with the refrain: "When Jesus finished . . ." (7:28; 11:1; 13:53; 19:1; 26:1). Another formula appears at the beginning and at the midpoint of Matthew's story: "From that time Jesus began . . ." (4:17; 16:21). Matthew sometimes repeats the same words of Jesus (5:29–30 = 18:8–9; 16:19 = 18:18).

Matthew also edits Mark by omitting concrete details and ordering the parts around a center. For example, his account of the storm at sea moves in a concentric pattern: a–b–c–b′–a′ (8:23–27). Jesus and the disciples in the boat (vs. 23) are contrasted with the men, the non-disciples on the shore (vs. 27). The great storm is contrasted with the great calm that results from Jesus' action (vss. 24 and 26b). At the center sits the dialogue between Jesus and the disciples. Matthew draws our attention to the core of the story: "Save us, Lord: we are perishing!" . . . "Why are you afraid, O men of little faith?" (vss. 25–26a).

At times Matthew also orders larger sections of his

story around a central event. A clear example is the section concerning bread (14:1–16:12):

Introduction
14:1–12   John the Baptist

First Series of Episodes
a 14:13–21   Feeding Five Thousand
b 14:22–33   Dismissal of Crowds/Walking on the Water
c 14:34–36   Signs and Healings in Gennesaret
d 15:1–20   Dispute with the Pharisees and Instructions for the Disciples

15:21–28 THE CANAANITE WOMAN'S FAITH (central episode)

Second Series of Episodes
a′ 15:29–38   Feeding Four Thousand
b′ 15:39   Dismissal of Crowds/Journey Across the Lake
c′ 16:1–4   Sign Refused to the Pharisees
d′ 16:5–12   Instructions for the Disciples About the Pharisees

Matthew's characters are more universal than Mark's. He more carefully delineates the differences between the suppliants, the followers, the crowds, and the Jewish religious authorities. In this story, Peter is the only follower who speaks directly to Jesus. Whether round, flat, or stock, these characters become more easily identified and associated with the actors in the real-life story of Matthew's community.

With this editorial work, Matthew has created a story that is more orderly, more universal, and more structured than Mark's. Because Matthew's story about Jesus was easily remembered, it served his community at Antioch in their liturgical gatherings and on their mission to all the nations. The story continued to shape the Christian movement long after the evangelist's death. It soon became known as the book of the church.

We question Matthew the evangelist one last time: "Did the Holy Spirit play a role in your work? If so, what was the Holy Spirit's role? How should we receive your story?"

Matthew replies: "My story was the product of the process I have described. I believe that the Holy Spirit was at work throughout that entire process. We listened to our experience, to the inherited traditions about Jesus, and to the broader Jewish-Hellenistic culture. In prayer and reflection we let what we heard come together, and we gradually reshaped the traditions into a story that would deepen our faith, give us hope, and strengthen our love. The Holy Spirit was our inspiration and our guide.

"I suggest that you receive our story as it was produced. Our good news was generated within and for a faith-filled community of men and women, children and adults, who believed in Jesus Christ. You also believe in Jesus Christ. We struggled to find meaning in uncertain times, as you struggle in your uncertain times. I suggest that you do what we did. Our story about Jesus is one of your traditions. Receive it individually and in community. Listen to it. Pray with it. Study it. Listen also to your unique experience in your culture. As you reflect and pray together, let what you hear live in you. If God so wishes, the product of that process will be an event in your lives that resembles what happened when we created our new story about Jesus. Through the same Holy Spirit, God will, I trust, enable you to capture the vision in the story, to discover its values, and to bring its vision and values into the decisions you make about how to live as Christians in your world."

We Christians believe that Matthew's story about Jesus is inspired, as are all the writings in the Hebrew and the Christian scriptures. A medieval painting that portrays the evangelist Matthew reflects how many people imagine the action of the Holy Spirit. In that picture a venerable old man with flowing beard and bald head bends over a writing desk on which rests a large parchment scroll. The evangelist is not alone. A classic angel with wings and flowing white garment stands beside him, one arm around the evangelist's shoulder and the other firmly guiding his hand as words flow from a quill pen. A heavenly glow illumines the face of Matthew and the angelic messenger. As Matthew writes, the angel represents the divine guidance and inspiration that makes his story the word of God.

We have no problem believing in Matthew's story as the word of God. However, we know that the evangelist was not a secretary responding to divine dictation and that his story did not drop from heaven. Matthew's gospel was the product of a much richer and more complex human process. The Holy Spirit guided this process. We call this guidance *inspiration*. The Spirit's guidance was as extensive and diffuse as the long process we have traced for the development of Matthew's story. The Holy Spirit guided not only the evangelist but also the individuals and communities that shaped and reshaped the traditions about Jesus. The Spirit empowered the Christian movement in its widespread activities of preaching and teaching as well as in its prayer and reflection at liturgical gatherings. The Spirit led the young Christian communities as they worked to remember Jesus' words and actions and to find meaning in them for their lives. The Spirit moved those communities to seek and find in Jesus' words and works the abiding presence of their risen Lord. The Spirit authorized certain members of those communities to write down their memories, and that same Spirit inspired Matthew the evangelist as he produced the story we read as his gospel.

As we read and pray with Matthew's story of Jesus, as we reflect on its meaning in our liturgy and announce its message to our world, that same Spirit guides us. Matthew and his community worked with *inherited traditions,* attended to their *present experience,* and responded to their *surrounding culture.* We must do the same. Matthew's story is our *inherited tradition.* As we listen to it in personal or community settings, we also listen to our *present experience* and our *contemporary culture.* We, too, must let what we hear come together in reflection and prayer so that we can discover how God through Matthew's story might be enabling us to live as Christians in our uncertain times.

We have described Matthew's story. With historical imagination we have reconstructed Matthew's uncertain times, relating them to our own. We have also read Matthew's story about Jesus of Nazareth, and we began to pray with that story. Finally, we interviewed Matthew the evangelist. With respect for the distance in time and the differences in culture that separate us from Matthew and his community, we have created a conversation based on the fact that we both live in uncertain times and believe that Jesus Christ is our risen Lord. We have combined historical information, literary analysis, psychological insights, and Christian faith to create a religious perspective that can hold together the historical world behind Matthew's story, the literary world in the story, and the world into which the story leads those who take it seriously as the inspired word of God. Now we will study that story more carefully by walking through it.

Reflection Questions

Before moving on, however, you might want to take some time with these questions:

- What is your impression of Matthew the evangelist?
- What insights or questions does the interview raise for you?
- How have you been inspired by the Holy Spirit?
- How does the Holy Spirit act in your life?
- What does *inspiration* mean to you?

Readings

L. Doohan, *Matthew: Spirituality for the 80's and 90's.* Santa Fe: Bear and Company, 1986, pages 7–27.

D. Senior, *Jesus.* Dayton: Pflaum, 1970, pages 5–27.

PART 2

Studying Matthew's Story

As we *study* Matthew's story section by section, we want to enter more deeply into its world to discover its message. To do this, we will pay close attention to how the plot moves and how the characters develop. We will also attend carefully to the five discourses that present the teaching of Jesus. As we study, we will imagine how Matthew's community let his gospel interact with the story of their experience in uncertain times. With reflection questions, we will then imagine how Matthew's story of Jesus might relate to our own uncertain times, leading us to new perspectives on our experience in today's world.

Our method can be called *composition criticism.* We combine historical information about Matthew's world with literary analysis of the narrative in his story about Jesus. But we do not compare his story with the parallel stories in Mark and Luke. Nor do we explain, as commentaries do, the meaning and background of key words and phrases. Instead, we concentrate on the story as a story composed by Matthew the evangelist both for the Christian community of Jews and Gentiles in Antioch around A.D. 85 and for us today.

Our method resembles *redaction criticism* in that we take seriously the world behind the text, that is, the concrete historical situation of Matthew and his community in Antioch. It differs from redaction criticism in that we focus on the entire story as a narrative, rather than on how the evangelist edited Mark, Q, and his other sources.

Our method is also like *narrative criticism* in that we focus on the narrative world within the text. It differs from narrative criticism in that we relate the story to the historical world of Matthew and his community.

Our method is also related to *form criticism* in that we identify literary forms within the narrative such as miracle stories, parables, and conflict stories. It differs from form criticism in that we do not trace the history of those forms through Matthew's sources to the earliest oral and written traditions about Jesus. We also refrain from forming judgments about how Matthew's story relates to the historical Jesus.

Finally, our approach moves beyond current historical-critical methods to imagine the world in front of the text, that is, the world into which studying Matthew's story in its historical situation can lead contemporary readers. Insights from modern psychology invite us to enter Matthew's story through active imagination. Our Christian faith invites us to expect God to meet us in that story through prayer. We combine, therefore, historical information, literary analysis, psychological insights, and Christian faith to create a religious perspective that can hold together the world behind Matthew's story, the world in the story, and the world into which the story can lead all those who take it seriously as the inspired word of God.

Reflection Questions

- Have you studied Matthew's story of Jesus? Was your study a positive or a negative experience? What

made it a positive experience? Or why was it negative?
- Complete the following statement: "Right now my
relationship to Matthew's story is best described
as . . ."

Readings

For an excellent discussion of the worlds behind, in,
and in front of biblical stories, see J. Shea, "Using Scripture in Pastoral Settings," *Chicago Studies* 23 (1984)
131–139.

In studying Matthew's story you may also want to
compare it with the parallel stories in Mark and Luke. An
excellent tool for this comparison: *Gospel Parallels: A Syn-
opsis of the First Three Gospels.* New York: Thomas Nelson
and Sons, 1981.

You may also want fuller explanation of particular
words and phrases, as well as their background in the Hebrew Scriptures. An excellent commentary is J.P. Meier,
Matthew. Wilmington: Michael Glazier, 1980. Other commentaries are listed in the "Selected Bibliography."

5

Infancy Narrative:
Story in Miniature
(1:1–2:23)

Matthew begins his story with a long list of names from Abraham, the father of Israel, through David and the kings of Judah, to Joseph, the father of Jesus (1:1–17). He divides the history of Israel into three periods: from Abraham to David, from David to the exile, and from the exile to Jesus the Christ. Four women—Tamar, Rahab, Ruth, and Bathsheba—are included as examples of how unexpected, even scandalous, events are included in God's plan for Israel.

With this genealogy, the evangelist asserts that Jesus is rooted in the people of Israel and that he is the Christ, the messiah, the goal of Israel's long history since its origin in Abraham. Jesus is the son of Abraham to whom God promised that all the nations of the earth would be blessed (Gen 22:18). He is the son of David, Israel's king whose messianic line can be traced through the kings of Judah both before and after the time of exile in Babylon. Matthew ends his genealogy with Joseph: "and Jacob the father of Joseph, the husband of Mary, of whom Jesus was born is called Christ" (1:16).

Another scandalous event! Joseph receives a dream about Mary's pregnancy and about what to name her child (1:18–25). According to Jewish custom, Mary's betrothal to

Joseph meant that they were married but not yet living together. When Mary shows herself to be with child, Joseph faces a painful dilemma. God resolves this conflict by revealing to Joseph in a dream that Mary has conceived by the Holy Spirit, that her child will be a son, and that he is to be named Jesus, because he will save Israel from its sins. Trusting the message without understanding it, Joseph accepts Jesus as his son and makes him a descendant of David. Since he is Joseph's son, Jesus can be the Christ, the messiah, the son of David. Since he is conceived by the Holy Spirit, he is also called Emmanuel—God-with-us.

After a star reveals to Gentile astrologers in the east that a king is born to the Jews, these wise men journey to pay him homage (2:1–12). When the magi arrive in Jerusalem, Herod directs them to Bethlehem. They follow the star to the place where they find the child with Mary, his mother. The wise men fall down and worship the child, offering him gold, frankincense, and myrrh. Being warned by God in a dream, the astrologers do not report back to Herod but return to the east by a route that does not take them through Jerusalem. Because of them the news about Jesus reaches the non-Jewish world to the east.

Herod seeks to kill the newborn king of the Jews. But in a dream God directs Joseph to flee with Jesus and his mother into Egypt (2:13–23). Joseph does what he is commanded. Herod orders that all the male children in Bethlehem be killed. Later God tells Joseph in a dream to leave Egypt and return to Palestine. Again Joseph acts according to God's word. Also in a dream, God tells Joseph not to settle in Bethlehem but to go north to Nazareth in Galilee, since Herod's son Archelaus is ruling Judea. By sojourning in Egypt, Jesus, Mary, and Joseph reenact two events of Jewish history—Joseph's sojourn in Egypt as steward to the Pharaoh and the exodus of the Hebrew slaves from Egypt to the land of promise in Palestine.

Matthew cites the Hebrew scriptures to show how each event of Jesus' infancy fits into God's overall plan for Israel. The evangelist introduces each citation with a formula: "All this took place to fulfill what the Lord had spoken by the prophet" (1:22). "This was to fulfill what the Lord had spoken by the prophet" (2:15). "Then was fulfilled what was spoken by the prophet Jeremiah" (2:17). "That what was spoken by the prophet might be fulfilled" (2:23). These explicit citations, as well as more indirect references, associate Jesus with the sacred traditions of Judaism and suggest that he is firmly rooted in the collective experience of God's chosen people.

Matthew reminds his community that they are rooted in Jesus Christ and through him in Abraham. Both the Jewish and the Gentile members can be sure that the history of Israel is their history. Since their present uncertain times continue that history, they can look to the events of Jesus' infancy and to the Hebrew scriptures behind them for guidance and meaning.

These events also deal with important questions: Who is Jesus? How can he be the messiah, the son of David, when he was conceived through the Holy Spirit? How was he the son of Abraham for both Jews and Gentiles? How did he get from David's city of Bethlehem in Judea, where he was born, to Nazareth in Galilee? Matthew shows different pieces that fit together into the mysterious plan to save the world that God revealed in the Old Testament.

Herod rejects Jesus; the magi accept Jesus. In these events, Matthew's community see a reflection of their own experience. In Herod they see the Pharisees at Jamnia who expelled them from the Jewish synagogues; in the magi they see the Gentiles who continued to join the Christian movement in Antioch.

Reflection Questions

- What are your family roots? How have they influenced your faith life?
- How do you treat people who are outsiders? How does the parish community treat them? Who are considered outsiders? Does this treatment need changing? How?
- Who is hostile to you because you believe in Jesus? How do you deal with their hostility?
- Have you ever been a sojourner in a foreign land? Literally or figuratively? What did you think? How did you feel?
- What scriptures do you cite to ground you in uncertain times? Make a list of them. How do they work?

Readings

For the best treatment of these chapters see R.E. Brown, *The Birth of the Messiah.* Garden City: Doubleday, 1977.

6

John the Baptist and Jesus in the Judean Desert (3:1–4:11)

A dramatic leap! A fresh start! A new time—the eschatological time! A new place—the wilderness of Judea! A new cast of characters—John the Baptist, Sadducees and Pharisees, an adult Jesus, his Father's voice, and Satan! Thus we move from Jesus' infancy to his adult baptism. Matthew says nothing about the time between Jesus' return to Nazareth and John's ministry at the Jordan. The mission of Jesus begins.

Preaching in the wilderness of Judea, John the Baptist washes the people of Israel in a baptism for the remission of sins (3:1–12). A prophet like Elijah and Isaiah, he announces, "Repent, for the kingdom of heaven is at hand" (3:2). His garments and food suggest that a time of urgent expectation has dawned, a time that asks for repentance. John's voice cries in the wilderness: "Prepare the way of the Lord, make straight his paths" (Is 40:3).

From Jerusalem and all Judea, crowds flock to John at the Jordan to confess their sins and to be baptized. But when Pharisees and Sadducees also come, John lashes out, "You brood of vipers! Who has warned you to flee from the wrath to come?" John warns them against being complacent just because they are descendants of Abraham. He admonishes them to bear fruit that befits this urgent time of repentance.

Next, John speaks about the messiah who is to come after him. John insists that the messiah will be greater than himself. He knows that his baptism is a water-ritual that invites people to repent but that the messiah will baptize Israel with a purifying fire and with the power of the Holy Spirit. As the messiah's servant, John is not worthy to even carry his sandals. When he comes, however, the messiah will gather good wheat into his barn and burn the chaff in unquenchable fire.

When Jesus comes to John to be baptized in the Jordan, God reveals the Nazarene to be the anointed messiah (3:13–17). Recognizing Jesus, John resists baptizing him and says, "I need to be baptized by you, and do you come to me?" Jesus responds: "Let it be so for now; for thus it is fitting to fulfill all righteousness." John then baptizes Jesus.

Immediately the heavens open. Jesus sees the Spirit of God descending like a dove, and God's voice is heard: "This is my beloved Son, with whom I am well pleased." God speaks to John and Jesus, to the crowds who came to be baptized, and to the Pharisees and Sadducees. God reveals to Israel that Jesus is anointed by the Holy Spirit to be their long-awaited messiah.

The Holy Spirit leads Jesus into the wilderness to confront Satan (4:1–11). After forty days without food, Jesus responds to the taunts hurled at him by Satan. First, Satan says, "If you are the Son of God, command these stones to become loaves of bread." Jesus answers with the Hebrew scriptures: "It is written, 'Man shall not live by bread alone, but by every word that proceeds from the mouth of God.' " Leading him to a high place in the temple area, Satan next challenges Jesus to test God's fidelity by throwing himself to the ground. Again Jesus cites words from scripture to assert that he trusts his Father.

On a very high mountain, Satan taunts Jesus a third time. Showing him all the nations of the world, he says: "All these I will give you, if you will fall down and worship me." But Jesus again wins the struggle: "Begone, Satan! for it is written, 'You shall worship the Lord your God and him only shall you serve.'" With these victories over Satan, Jesus reverses what Israel did to God on their journey through the desert to the promised land. By asking for food and water and worshiping false idols, Israel tested God (Dt 6–8). In the desert, Jesus reenacts Israel's struggle with evil. By resisting similar temptations, Jesus demonstrates that he is the true Son in whom God's power over Satan is at work in the world.

In these events, John announces the reign of heaven and warns about impending judgment; Jesus is revealed to be God's Son who is empowered by the Holy Spirit; and Jesus conquers Satan. Matthew's community sees in these events that God has once again begun to act in the world to save the chosen people of Israel. Israel believed that the God who created the world continually acted in that world. This God rescued Israel from slavery in Egypt, helped them survive the desert, led them to settle in the promised land, and instructed them to build a temple on Mount Zion.

In the Babylonian exile, that same God inspired Isaiah, Jeremiah, and Ezekiel to interpret those harsh events as God's judgment on Israel for their infidelity. But God also promised to deliver them from their Assyrian and Babylonian captors, so that they might return to their land and rebuild their temple in Jerusalem. When Jesus comes to John to be baptized at the Jordan, when he confronts Satan in the wilderness, Matthew's community recognizes that God's reign, God's kingly power over the world, is revealed anew to Israel in Jesus their Messiah.

Reflection Questions

- What events and persons reveal God's power to you? How do you respond?
- What similarities do you see between Jesus' struggles with evil and your own? Do you want to dialogue with Jesus about these struggles?

Readings

For a thorough study of John the Baptist see J.P. Meier, "John the Baptist in Matthew's Gospel," *Journal of Biblical Literature* 99 (1980) 283–405.

7

Jesus Preaches, Teaches, and Heals in Galilee (4:12–7:28)

Another fresh start! Another new setting! Another new cast of characters! When Herod puts John the Baptist in prison, his preaching and baptizing at the Jordan ends. Then Jesus begins preaching, teaching, and healing in Galilee of the Gentiles. People follow Jesus; enemies confront him. Crowds flock to him with their sick; men and women beg to be cured. With John in prison, Jesus now begins his mission to Israel, and Israel reacts to his words and actions.

After John the Baptist is arrested, Jesus moves from his home in Nazareth to Capernaum by the sea to begin his public work (4:12–17). Again Matthew cites the Hebrew scriptures to show that Jesus is meant to work in "Galilee of the Gentiles" (Is 8:22–9:2). Light comes to Jews and Gentiles in Galilee when Jesus announces what John had announced in the Judean desert: "Repent, for the kingdom of heaven is at hand" (4:17).

Jesus next calls four fishermen (4:18–22). He invites Simon and Andrew by saying, "Follow me and I will make you fishers of men." The two men leave their nets to walk after Jesus. James and John hear Jesus call them, and they also respond: "Immediately they left the boat and their father, and followed him." Following Jesus must mean that they leave their family and their fishing to travel with Jesus as his companions. Jesus initiates the call, but that gift demands an immediate response, a radical commitment, and an abrupt change of life-style.

Matthew summarizes Jesus' work in Galilee with these words: "And he went about all Galilee, teaching in their synagogues and preaching the gospel of the kingdom and healing every disease and every infirmity among the people" (4:23). Having heard Jesus preach (4:17), we are now prepared both to listen to his teaching in the sermon on the mount (5:1–7:28) and to watch him heal the sick and possessed (8:1–9:34).

Jesus works in Galilee of the Gentiles, but his fame spreads throughout Syria. From all four corners of the Roman province—from Galilee in the northwest, from the Decapolis in the northeast, from Jerusalem and Judea in the southwest, and from Perea beyond the Jordan in the southeast, from everywhere but Samaria, crowds of Jews and Gentiles flock to hear Jesus, to touch him, to beg his healing. The crowds bring their sick, and Jesus heals their pain and disease. He cures demoniacs, epileptics, and paralytics too.

Seeing the crowds, Jesus climbs a mountain and sits down. He calls the four fishermen to gather round. Then he teaches both them and the crowds. We call his discourse the sermon on the mount (5:1–7:28). Matthew has selected and arranged these sayings according to the following plan:

- Setting: Crowds and Followers (5:1–2)
- Prologue: Beatitudes/Good Works (5:3–16)
- The Jewish Law (5:17–48)
- Exterior Display: Almsgiving, Praying, and Fasting (6:1–18)
- Concern and Unconcern (6:19–7:12)

- Epilogue: Discerning and Choosing/Rewards and Punishments (7:13–27)
- Reaction: Crowds (7:28)

The beatitudes (5:3–12) name inner values, attitudes, and dispositions called for in the good news about the reign of God and its vision. Living out the call to repent means being poor in spirit and being meek—knowing our need for God. Jesus calls his listeners to mourn those who turn away from God, to hunger and thirst to do God's will, to be merciful toward others, to keep their hearts dedicated to God, to work to make peace, and to take an active part in God's work of reconciliation. Choosing God as the center of their lives, those who live these values are happy now, for they already know that in the future they will see God, as children see their Father. In the reign of God they will be fully satisfied.

Next, Jesus addresses his hearers: "Blessed are you when men revile you and persecute you and utter all kinds of evil against you falsely on my account. Rejoice and be glad, for your reward is great in heaven, for so men persecuted the prophets who were before you" (5:11–12). He goes on to say that those who live these beatitudes are like salt that flavors and preserves or like a light that illuminates a house (5:13–16). Matthew's community reflects on these beatitudes as they experience persecution both from Jamnia Pharisees and from Rome with the internal dissension it caused.

The Jewish Law (5:17–48)

Jesus next speaks about the Jewish law (5:17–20). He has come not to abolish that law but to fulfill it by teaching its true interpretation. The law, which will not pass away

until all is accomplished, demands a righteousness surpassing that of the scribes and Pharisees. Elsewhere Jesus
names the law's basic demand: "You shall love the Lord
your God with all your heart, and with all your soul, and
with all your mind. This is the great and first commandment. And a second is like it. You shall love your neighbor
as yourself" (22:37–39). Love is the center of the Jewish
law. Those who seek the reign of God are to express that
love by their actions toward God and others, toward themselves, and toward the world.

By applying this love-command to six specific statements in the Jewish law, Jesus next shows how love informs both inner attitudes and external actions (5:21–48).
Jews have always heard that killing another or committing
adultery is wrong. But Jesus also condemns an anger that
wants to kill or a lust that wants to violate a woman. Jews
have heard in the law that the man who divorces his wife
must give her the required certificate, but Jesus says that
his action makes both his wife and the man who marries
her adulterers.

The law also prohibits false oaths, but Jesus forbids all
oath-taking. Inviting his hearers to respond to violence
with non-violent actions, Jesus condemns the Jewish
practice of retaliation. Finally, Jews have heard that they
should love their neighbor and hate their enemy, but Jesus
teaches that love should extend also to one's enemies and
that people should do good to those who hate them. With
each statement, Jesus uses the love-command to go beyond
its demands, to qualify its meaning, or to replace it with
another statement. He then states the ideal: "You, therefore, must be perfect, as your heavenly Father is perfect" (5:48).

Hearing Jesus' words about the Jewish law, Matthew's
community recognizes that he, not the Pharisees at Jamnia, is their authoritative rabbi. He reinterprets the law

around the central value of love. Now they must decide how to live that love in a community which is torn by dissension and where love for one another has grown cold.

Jesus next teaches what the surpassing righteousness of the kingdom demands with regard to traditional acts of Jewish piety—almsgiving, praying, and fasting (6:1–18). He states: "Beware of practicing your piety before men in order to be seen by them; for then you will have no reward from your Father who is in heaven." He contrasts the grandiose style of those he calls hypocrites to the simple style of those who practice their piety in secret, so as to be rewarded by their Father in heaven. He also teaches the Our Father, the central prayer of the kingdom. He then comments on the need to forgive: "For if you forgive men their trespasses, your heavenly Father also will forgive you; but if you do not forgive men their trespasses, neither will your Father forgive your trespasses" (6:14–15). Matthew's community hears these words as a call to look at their need to forgive and be reconciled to one another.

Concern and Unconcern (6:19–7:12)

Next, Jesus teaches that the kingdom demands single-hearted dedication (6:19–34). The reign of God, which asks for clear choices between treasures on earth and treasures in heaven, between money and God, wants the eye to be sound so that the entire body will be filled with light. Jesus insists that whoever chooses to live by the kingdom should be free of worldly care and anxiety. Like birds in the air or lilies in the field, they are to make God, rather than human needs for shelter, food, and clothing, the center of their concern. Jesus concludes: "Seek first his kingdom and his righteousness, and all those things shall be yours as well" (6:33). In their uncertain times, Matthew's community hears Jesus' words addressed to their lack of trust and their anxieties about surviving.

Jesus then teaches the double-command to love God and neighbor (7:7–12). He assures his listeners that whoever seeks God in prayer and knocks at God's door can expect that God will find them and grant what they ask. But they must also act: "So whatever you wish that men would do to you, do so to them; for this is the law and the prophets" (7:12). He teaches his listeners that authentic prayer leads to concrete action toward others; this action must in turn be rooted in prayer.

Finally, Jesus tells his hearers how to choose what is right and wrong, and he describes the rewards and punishments for those choices (7:13–27). Choosing God's reign means rejecting the easy way that leads to destruction. Thus, the faithful enter the narrow gate and walk the hard way that leads to life. Embracing God's reign also means keeping an eye out for false prophets and recognizing them by their fruits. Jesus continues: "Not every one who says to me, 'Lord, Lord,' shall enter the kingdom of heaven, but he who does the will of my Father who is in heaven" (7:21). He declares that a wise man hears and acts out Jesus' words because they disclose his Father's will. Jesus assures his listeners that this man's house withstands rain and floods because it is built on rock. In contrast, Jesus asserts that the foolish man, hearing his words, does not carry them into action. His house falls in the storm because it is built on sand. Matthew's community hears these words as a challenge to recommit themselves to the reign of God.

Matthew concludes his account of the sermon on the mount by describing the crowd's reaction: "And when Jesus finished these sayings, the crowds were astonished at his teaching. For he taught them as one who had authority, and not as their scribes" (7:28). Jesus teaches the crowds of Jews and Gentiles and the four fishermen who followed him that to live according to the kingdom means hearing and doing the will of their Father in heaven. God's will is that they love God and neighbor, themselves and their world, and that they express their love in prayer and action. Jesus promises that rewards for such a surpassing righteousness will be great in heaven.

As Matthew's community hears the sermon on the mount, they do not consider it a new code of law to replace the old Jewish law. Nor do they see it as an impossible ideal to be kept in view or a set of extraordinary demands for the short time until Jesus' second coming at the end of the age. Receiving Jesus' teaching as a revelation of the values of God's reign, they ask God to empower them so that they may live according to those values in their uncertain times.

Reflection Questions

- Does Jesus call you to repent at this time? If so, what does *repentance* mean? How will you repent?
- Rewrite the beatitudes to fit your family, your parish, your neighborhood, your city: "Blessed are the . . . for they will . . ."
- Has love grown cold in your communities—at home, at church, at work, with God? How can you better live the love-command?
- What does giving alms, praying, and fasting mean in today's world? Do you need to create a space for God in your life by fasting from the media, from the stress of the fast pace?
- What anxieties prevent you from being dedicated with a single-heartedness to God's reign? Can you ask God to help you grow in trust?
- How do you mix prayer and action in your daily life?

Are you happy with the mix? What would you like it to be?
- What choices are you making at this time? How will you make them? Will God be part of the process?
- Is God inviting you to accept anew the values in Jesus' sermon on the mount? How do you respond?

Readings

For a thorough study of the sermon on the mount see J. Lambrecht, *The Sermon on the Mount.* Wilmington: Michael Glazier, 1986.

8

Jesus Preaches, Teaches, and Heals in Galilee (8:1–9:34)

Matthew next tells how Jesus healed every disease and every infirmity throughout Galilee (8:1–9:34). In these miracle stories three elements occur in the same order: *circumstances, miracle,* and *aftermath.* When Jesus cures the leper, for example, the circumstances are described (8:1–2), then the cure is recounted (8:3), and then the aftermath is described (8:4). This pattern can be found in the other miracle-stories:

	Circumstances	Miracle	Aftermath
Centurion's Servant	8:5–12	8:13	—
Peter's Mother-in-Law	8:14	8:15ab	8:15c
Stilling the Storm	8:23–25	8:26	8:27
Gerasene Demoniac	8:28	8:29–32	8:33–34
Paralytic	9:1–2a	9:2b–6	9:7
Jairus' Daughter	9:18–19, 23–24	9:25	9:26
Woman with the Issue of Blood	9:20–21	9:22a	9:22b
Two Blind Men	9:27	9:28–29	9:30–31
A Dumb Demoniac	9:32	9:33a	9:33b–34

In healing a leper, the Roman centurion's servant, and Peter's mother-in-law, Jesus reveals his power over physical illness (8:1–17). The centurion speaks his conviction about Jesus' power: "Lord, I am not worthy to have you come under my roof; but only say the word, and my servant will be healed." And Jesus commends this Gentile: "Not even in Israel have I found such faith." Matthew then associates these healings with Isaiah's words about the servant of the Lord: "He took our infirmities and bore our diseases" (Is 53:4). Gentile members in Matthew's community identify with the Roman centurion.

Discipleship (8:18–9:17)

As night descends, Jesus commands the Galilean crowd of Jews and Gentiles who have heard his teaching to make the dangerous journey across the Sea of Galilee (8:18–22). A scribe volunteers: "Teacher, I will follow you wherever you go." But Jesus tempers his enthusiasm by saying, "Foxes have holes, and birds of the air have nests; but the Son of Man has nowhere to lay his head." When a disciple requests: "Lord, let me first go and bury my father," Jesus responds: "Follow me, and leave the dead to bury their own dead." Following Jesus demands more than listening to him teach and watching him heal the sick. Followers must be ready to share all that is implied in the fact that Jesus has no place to lay his head. They must risk casting their lot with Jesus. They must even put aside the legitimate but conflicting demands of Jewish familial piety. Simeon ben Eliezar and the other Jews in Matthew's community relate Jesus' words to their own struggle to remain loyal both to their families and to the Christian community in Antioch.

Matthew next shows Jesus getting into a boat. The disciples follow him while the crowd remains on the shore. On the lake they encounter a storm. As the boat is tossed by the waves, Jesus sleeps. His disciples wake him by pleading, "Save us, Lord; we are perishing." Jesus rebukes them: "Why are you afraid, O men of little faith?" His followers have enough faith to risk following him into the boat for a night journey across the lake. But they do not trust that he will keep them from perishing in the storm. Theirs is a faith that can still know fear. Jesus then reveals his power over nature by calming the storm. On the shore the crowds marvel: "What sort of man is this, that even winds and sea obey him?" (8:23–27). Matthew's community relates this event to the storms in their own lives.

Across the lake, Jesus heals two demoniacs in the non-Jewish land of the Gadarenes (8:28–34). The two come out of the tombs, block Jesus' way to the city, and cry: "What have you to do with us, O Son of God?" Jesus commands the evil spirits to leave the two men and to go into the nearby swine. When the spirits do so, the swine rush down the hillside and perish in the water, as the spirits return to their home at the bottom of the lake. After herdsmen spread the word, the people beg Jesus to leave their land. The time for his mission outside Galilee has not yet arrived.

Back in Galilee, men bring a paralytic to Jesus, and he responds: "Take heart, my son; your sins are forgiven." When scribes interpret his words as blasphemy, Jesus asserts his power over sin by commanding the paralytic to take up his bed and go home. Frightened, the crowds glorify God for having given such authority to a man (9:1–8).

Next, Jesus calls a tax collector named Matthew, eats a meal in his house, and reacts to those who question his actions (9:9–17). When the Pharisees ask his disciples why their teacher eats with tax collectors and sinners, Jesus responds: "I came not to call the righteous, but sinners." After disciples of John the Baptist ask why Jesus' disciples do not fast, Jesus predicts: "The days will come when the bridegroom is taken away from them, and then they will fast."

Models of Faith (9:18–31)

Jesus then heals the woman with the issue of blood and raises the daughter of Jairus from death to life. Jairus models faith by stating his conviction that Jesus can raise his daughter from the dead. On the way to his house, an invalid woman says to herself: "If I only touch his garment, I shall be made well." Jesus says to her: "Take heart, daughter, your faith has made you well." At Jairus' house, Jesus takes the hand of the man's daughter, and she rises back to life. Matthew comments: "And the report of this went through all that district" (9:18–26).

Finally, Jesus heals two blind men and a dumb demoniac (9:27–34). As his fame continues to spread throughout Galilee, the crowds marvel: "Never was anything like this seen in Israel." But the Pharisees react with hostility: "He casts out demons by the prince of demons."

Since medicine was primitive in Jesus' day, the blind and the lame, the lepers and the possessed were pushed to the margins of their society because people considered them to be victims of cosmic evil power represented by Satan. The blind and the lame beg for coins from passers-by as they enter or leave their villages. Lepers wander the countryside in bands to avoid human contact with anyone other than their fellow lepers. Wild epileptics and psychotics roam among tombs, shrieking like animals. When Jesus shows compassion on those outcasts by healing them, he confronts the evil power that grips them and reveals that God's power is present and active in the world. He also empowers these marginal and oppressed persons to live a normal life in their society.

Matthew has introduced us to the leading characters in his story. Jesus has begun to preach, teach, and heal in Galilee of the Gentiles. Peter and Andrew, James and John, and then Matthew have left their work to follow Jesus, and with others they have risked following him into a boat and into a storm on the treacherous Sea of Galilee. Ready to accept that Jesus has no place to call home, they put their commitment to him ahead of family loyalties. Matthew's community recognize their own challenges and struggles in those of Jesus' followers.

Other men and women are suppliants who recognize their needs, who are convinced that Jesus has the power to meet their needs, and who express that conviction in word and action. Somehow they sense that God's reign is present and active in Jesus. Jesus rewards their faith by using God's power to heal their diseases and to cast out demons. Matthew invites his community to see themselves in these suppliants.

Jews and Gentiles—the Galilean crowds—flock to Jesus with their sick. They marvel at his power to teach and heal. But the scribes and Pharisees, the Jewish religious authorities, challenge Jesus by stating that an evil power is at work in his healings and exorcisms. Matthew's community identifies Jesus' enemies with their own enemies and the crowds with those Jews and Gentiles in Antioch who marvel at their commitment but choose not to join the community.

Reflection Questions

- What does following Jesus demand of you? Has it ever involved conflict with other loyalties? How did you resolve the conflict?

- Recall storms in your life! Were they a call to deeper faith?
- Are you a suppliant—aware of your hurts and those of our world and convinced that the risen Jesus has power to heal them? How do you express that conviction?

Readings

For further treatment of chapters 8–9, see W.G. Thompson, "Reflections on the Composition of Matthew 8:1–9:34," *Catholic Biblical Quarterly* (1971) 365–388.

9

Jesus and the Twelve Disciples: Mission to Israel (9:35–10:42)

After Jesus' activities in Galilee of the Gentiles, Matthew introduces the mission of his twelve disciples to Israel (9:35–10:4). He again summarizes Jesus' activities: "And Jesus went about all the cities and villages, teaching in their synagogues and preaching the gospel of the kingdom, and healing every disease and every infirmity" (9:35). Seeing the crowds, Jesus is moved with compassion. He calls his twelve disciples and shares with them his power to heal every disease and infirmity.

Next, Matthew names the twelve disciples. We do not know how or when they were chosen from the other disciples. But Matthew singles them out for the mission to Israel. He begins to attribute different tasks to different followers. The twelve disciples share Jesus' mission to Israel. Peter, the first named, is the sole spokesman for all the other disciples. Peter, James, and John witness Jesus' transfiguration and are closest to him in Gethsemane. Women witness his death and receive news of his resurrection. Followers include:

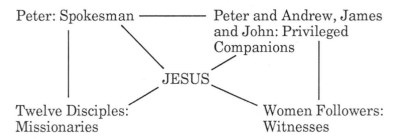

Peter: Spokesman ———— Peter and Andrew, James
and John: Privileged
Companions

JESUS

Twelve Disciples: Women Followers:
Missionaries   Witnesses

Matthew next recounts Jesus' discourse to the twelve disciples about their mission to Israel (10:5–42). The evangelist arranges this collection of predictions and instructions, judgments and promises, according to an orderly plan:

A   Commission; Instructions; Strategy (10:5–15)
B   Predictions: Opposition from Israel (10:16–25)
C   Exhortation: "Have no fear!" (10:26–33)
B'   Predictions: Division within Families (10:34–39)
A'   Promise: Rewards for Israel (10:40–42)

Commissioning the twelve disciples, Jesus instructs them about provisions and describes their missionary strategy (10:5–15). He tells them: "Go nowhere among the Gentiles, and enter no town of the Samaritans, but go rather to the lost sheep of the house of Israel" (10:5–6). Like their master, Jesus' disciples must limit their activities to the cities and towns in Galilee because now is the time for the mission to Israel. As they have heard Jesus preach, so they are to preach: "The kingdom of heaven is at hand." As they have watched Jesus heal, so they are to heal: "Heal the sick, raise the dead, cleanse lepers, cast out demons." Although Jesus has taught in the Jewish synagogues, his disciples are not to teach because he is the teacher and they are his disciples. Jesus entrusts his power with these twelve men as a gift, and they are to use that power for others without expecting payment.

Jesus next instructs his disciples about provisions and strategy for their mission to Israel (10:9–15). He tells them not to take money or clothes but to rely on the hospitality of those to whom they are sent, so that they might move with urgency. Jesus describes how the disciples are to enter a city or village, how they are to find the homes of those who are worthy, and how they are to leave that household or city when they are not received. He ends with a harsh word of condemnation for those who reject the disciples' mission: "It shall be more tolerable on the day of judgment for the land of Sodom and Gomorrah than for that town" (10:15).

Opposition (10:16–39)

Predicting that their fellow Jews will persecute the twelve disciples, Jesus instructs them on how to respond and associates their experience with his own persecution (10:16–25). He foretells that Jews will deliver the disciples over to their councils, flog them in their synagogues, and drag them before Gentile officials in Galilee. The disciples can even expect that their families will be hostile and everyone will hate them. Indeed, Israel will react to them as they have seen Israel react to their master and teacher. But

Jesus assures them: "You will not have gone through all the towns of Israel before the Son of Man comes" (10:23).

Next, Jesus exhorts the twelve disciples to have no fear because those who kill the body cannot kill the soul (10:26–33). After reminding them that their Father values them more than sparrows, Jesus assures the twelve disciples that he will acknowledge those who acknowledge him to his Father in heaven.

Jesus then predicts that the mission to Israel will cause division within Jewish families (10:34–39). His disciples are startled when Jesus says, "Do not think that I have come to bring peace on earth; I have not come to bring peace, but a sword." Jesus predicts that family members will be divided from family members and loyalties will be tested. Jesus' followers will be asked to take up their cross, to lose their lives to find them, even to renounce family loyalties when these conflict with loyalty to Jesus.

Jesus concludes with the promise that whoever in Israel receives the twelve disciples will be rewarded (10:40–42). As the Father is identified with Jesus who carries out God's mission, so Jesus is identified with the disciples who take part in that mission. He is sender in those being sent, master in his servants, teacher in his disciples. So those who receive his disciples receive both Jesus and his Father in heaven. Indeed, Jesus assures them, "Whoever gives to one of these little ones even a cup of cold water because he is a disciple, truly, I say to you, he shall not lose his reward" (10:42).

Hearing this discourse, Matthew's community in Antioch recalls what Jesus taught about single-hearted dedication to the reign of God and freedom from worldly cares and anxieties (6:19–34). Community members also recall how the four fishermen—Peter and Andrew, James and John—and Matthew the tax collector left their families and occupation to follow Jesus (4:18–22; 9:9) and how the disciples risked entering the boat with Jesus to cross the Sea of Galilee at night (8:18–27). They also hear echoes of the Pharisees' hostile reaction to Jesus' healing power (9:35).

As they reflect on Jesus' words, Matthew's community see his strong condemnation of Israel fulfilled when the Romans end the Jewish revolt in A.D. 70 by destroying Jerusalem and the temple. Subsequent conflicts with the Pharisees at Jamnia show the community in Antioch that Jesus' predictions about opposition from Israel have been fulfilled. The community also associates division within their own families with Jesus' predictions about conflicts between family loyalties and the demands of carrying out the mission to Israel. Jesus' instructions also carry lessons for their new mission to all the nations, that is, to both Jews and Gentiles in the Roman world.

Reflection Questions

- What is your mission today? What is the mission of your family, your church, your work? What are its limits?
- What does it cost to carry out this mission? How do you respond to the demands?
- Recall times when you have been in conflict with family members, with friends, with colleagues at work, with members of your parish. How did you manage the conflict?

Readings

For a more detailed analysis and discussion see D.R.A. Hare, *The Theme of Jewish Persecution of Christians in the Gospel According to St. Matthew.* Cambridge: Cambridge University Press, 1967.

For a discussion of "the twelve disciples" see S. Freyne, *The Twelve: Disciples and Apostles.* Kansas City: Sheed and Ward, 1968.

10

Israel Reacts; Jesus Teaches in Parables (11:1–13:58)

An event concerning John the Baptist and Jesus moves Matthew's story ahead. Using the formula that concludes each discourse, Matthew informs us that Jesus now resumes his own activities of preaching and teaching in the cities of Galilee (11:1). John, imprisoned by Herod Antipas, sends his disciples to Jesus with a question: "Are you he who is to come or shall we wait for another?" Jesus responds: "Go and tell John what you hear and see: the blind receive their sight and the lame walk, lepers are cleansed and the deaf hear, and the dead are raised up, and the poor have good news preached to them" (11:4–5). In saying this, Jesus summarizes both his own mission to Israel and that of his twelve disciples (4:12–10:42).

As John's disciples return to their master, Jesus identifies the Baptist as a prophet and more than a prophet, even as the greatest born of woman. Indeed John is Elijah, who was expected to return to prepare Israel for their messiah. John has announced the good news of God's reign (3:2). But still John is not as great as the least in that kingdom of heaven, for his imprisonment prevented him from seeing and hearing the kingdom revealed in Jesus' preaching, teaching, and healing throughout Galilee.

Jesus then rebukes the present generation of Israel,

comparing their demands to unreasonable children in the marketplace who are calling to their playmates. Jesus points out that John came neither eating nor drinking, and the people said: "He has a demon." However, when Jesus, the Son of Man, did eat and drink, these same contrary people declared, "Behold a glutton and a drunkard, a friend of tax collectors and sinners!" As Matthew's community at Antioch recalls the argument in Matthew's home (9:9–17), as well as earlier events with John and Jesus (3:1–17; 4:12–25), they relate this judgment of Israel to the destruction of Jerusalem and the temple.

Matthew next strings together a series of events without indicating the elapse of time or the movement from place to place (11:20–12:50). The evangelist focuses attention on Jesus as he evaluates various reactions to his messianic mission. Harsh judgments, attacks and counterattacks are mixed with prayer, healings, and a new definition of family. Matthew arranges these events in another concentric pattern:

A   Unrepentant Cities; Little Ones (11:20–30)
B   Pharisees: Debates and Plan (12:1–14)
C   Crowds: Jesus the Healing Servant (12:15–21)
B' Pharisees: Reaction to Cures (12:22–37)
A' Evil Generation; True Family (12:38–50)

In Chorazin, Bethsaida, and Capernaum, Jesus has announced the good news of the kingdom, taught in the synagogues in these cities in Galilee, and healed every disease and infirmity. But the townspeople fail to repent and believe that God's reign had indeed arrived. Now, Jesus condemns these towns and gives thanks for what has been revealed to little ones (11:20–30). He thanks his Father for letting simple persons see and hear, for letting them come

to know that his words and actions reveal his relation to
the Father. He invites others: "Come to me, all who labor
and are heavy-laden, and I will give you rest. Take my yoke
upon you, and learn from me; for I am gentle and lowly of
heart, and you will find rest for your souls. For my yoke is
easy, and my burden is light" (11:28–30). Hearing this,
Matthew's community remembers the beatitudes (5:3–12).

Next, the Pharisees confront Jesus about laws concerning behavior on the sabbath (12:1–14). First, his enemies challenge him about his followers who do forbidden
work by plucking and breaking open grain. Jesus declares
that he has been given authority over both the temple and
the sabbath. When the Pharisees then ask him whether
healing on the sabbath is lawful, Jesus refutes their argument and cures a man with a withered hand. Matthew
notes that now the Pharisees harden their opposition: "But
the Pharisees went out and took counsel against him, how
to destroy him" (12:14). Hearing this, the community in
Antioch wonders whether the Pharisees will succeed in
carrying out their plans against Jesus and identifies their
plotting with the plots of the Pharisees at Jamnia.

Crowds and Pharisees (12:15–37)

As time passes, Galilean crowds of Jews and Gentiles
continue to follow Jesus, and he heals their sick (12:15–21).
Matthew associates these healings with those of the servant of the Lord who with God's Spirit shall proclaim justice to the Gentiles and bring that justice to victory. In his
name, the Gentiles hope. Hearing this, Matthew's community recalls how Jesus' actions took place in Galilee of the
Gentiles (4:12–17) and how Jesus cured the Roman centurion's servant in Capernaum (8:5–13).

Jesus next heals a blind and dumb demoniac. Again,

the crowds are amazed, and the Pharisees say: "It is only by Beelzebul, the prince of demons, that this man casts out demons" (12:22–37). This reminds Matthew's listeners of the contrasting responses when Jesus healed a dumb man (9:32–34). But this time Jesus argues against the Pharisees' interpretation by saying that Satan cannot work against himself. Satan cannot cast out his own demons. Jesus insists that his healings reveal God's power at work in the world because God enables Jesus to bind the evil powers and plunder their dwelling places. In addition, Jesus declares that by choosing to stand against the power of God, the Pharisees have spoken a blasphemy against the Spirit of God that cannot be forgiven. With biting words, Jesus condemns the Pharisees for their evil speech, "You brood of vipers! How can you speak good, when you are evil? For out of the abundance of the heart the mouth speaks" (12:34). In this indictment, the community at Antioch hears echoes of John's harsh words to the Pharisees and Sadducees at the Jordan (3:7–12).

Now Jesus responds to the Pharisees' demand for a sign by condemning this evil generation of Israel. He then describes what being members of his true family means (12:38–50). He explains that the sign to be given to such an adulterous generation will resemble the sign of Jonah: "So will the Son of Man be three days and three nights in the heart of the earth" (12:40). This sign also implies that "the men of Nineveh" and "the Queen from the South" will rise up at the time of judgment to condemn this generation for failing to recognize that Jesus is greater than Jonah the prophet and Solomon the king of Israel. As Jesus promises to return to condemn this evil generation, Matthew's community wonders whether his predictions have not come to pass in the events of the Jewish revolt.

While Jesus speaks to the crowds and his followers inside a house, his mother and brothers stand outside and ask to speak to him. In response, Jesus defines his true family not as kin by blood but as those who are his disciples. Gesturing toward his followers, he says: "Here are my mother and my brothers! For whoever does the will of my Father in heaven is my brother, and sister, and mother" (12:49–50). Jesus' statement reminds Matthew's listeners that he called four fishermen and a tax collector to follow him (4:18–22; 9:9) and that he spoke of discipleship when he invited the crowds to cross the lake at night (8:18–22). His announcement also echoes his words in the sermon on the mount about doing the will of his Father in heaven (6:7–15: 7:21–27).

With this series of events, the community at Antioch sees Israel reacting to the missionary activities of Jesus and the twelve disciples, and Jesus responding to Israel's reactions. He warns Galilean towns, wins initial encounters with the Pharisees, and promises to condemn this evil generation at the time of judgment. However, Jesus continues to heal the sick brought to him by Galilean crowds, and those crowds continue to be amazed at his power. These events also show Jesus thanking his Father for revealing himself to little ones and describing his true family as disciples who do the will of their Father in heaven. As Matthew's community reflects on these different reactions to Jesus, they think about how different groups are reacting to them in their uncertain times.

Parables (13:1–52)

Matthew next presents Jesus' beautiful parable discourse (13:1–52). At the lakeshore, Jesus tells the crowds and his disciples simple, disarming stories so that they may see and understand the mysteries of God's reign. Inside a house, Jesus continues to teach and explain other parables to his disciples. Matthew again creates a well-ordered arrangement:

Part I: At the Lakeshore; Jesus, Crowds and Disciples (13:1–2)

A   Parable: The Sower (13:3–9)
B   Dialogue: Why Jesus Spoke in Parables (13:10–17)
A'   Explanation to the Disciples: The Sower (13:18–23)
C   Parable: Wheat and Weeds (13:24–30)
D   Double-Parable: Mustard Seed; Leaven (13:31–33)
E   Conclusion: Editorial Comment (13:34–35)

Part II: Inside the House: Jesus and Disciples (13:36)

C'   Explanation: Wheat and Weeds (13:37–43)
D'   Double-Parable: Money Buried in a Field; Pearl of Great Price (13:44–46)
F/F'   Parable and Explanation: Net Let Down into the Sea (13:47–50)
E'   Conclusion (13:51–52)

Parables, vivid or strange stories from nature or common life, tease us into thought. They have both a literal meaning and a deeper, more hidden meaning, for they tell us something about the mysterious reign of God. Jesus speaks in parables to bring about change in the crowds and in the disciples who have ears to hear. He wants them to make decisions that will enable them to live more in tune with God's reign.

In his parables Jesus sometimes describes habitual actions that occur in real life, such as farmers sowing seed in their fields or fishermen sorting out the fish in their nets. Other parables recount one-time events, such as finding a treasure buried in a field or buying a pearl of great price. Jesus also compares God's reign to such unlikely things as a grain of mustard seed or leaven hidden in flour.

At the Lakeshore (13:1–35)

In this discourse, Jesus begins with a story about a sower who sows seed in his field (13:3–9). Matthew's listeners needed to remember that Galilean farmers scatter seed before plowing it under the earth. In this story, the farmer expects a bad harvest because the seed sown on the path, on the rocks, and among the thorns will produce no grain. He is completely surprised when the seed sown on the small area of good ground yields an amazing harvest of thirty-, sixty-, and a hundred-fold. Hearing this story, Matthew's community reflects on their surprise that so many Gentiles have been attracted to the Christian movement.

Next, Jesus' disciples engage him in a private conversation about why he speaks to the crowds in parables (13:10–17). Jesus responds by distinguishing his followers from the crowds. He explains that God has given the disciples to know the secrets of God's reign. Jesus then expands his response by saying, "This is why I speak to them in parables, because seeing they do not see, and hearing they do not hear, nor do they understand. . . . But blessed are your eyes, for they see, and your ears, for they hear." This contrast that Jesus makes between the disciples and the crowds fits with what Matthew's community already knows about these characters.

Jesus then explains the parable of the sower to his disciples (13:18–23). He identifies the seed with "the word of the kingdom" and the path, rocks, thorns, and good ground with the persons who have heard that word. His explanation moves the emphasis in the parable from surprise at the unexpected harvest to the varied responses to the mission to Israel that Matthew has described (11:1–12:50).

Next Jesus tells the crowds and the disciples a story in which a householder sows wheat, but his enemy secretly scatters a poisonous weed among the wheat (13:24–30). At first the householder cannot distinguish the wheat from the weeds. When the differences become obvious, however, the servants expect the householder to instruct them to pull up the weeds. But their master surprises them by saying, "No, lest in gathering the weeds you root up the wheat along with them. Let both grow together until the harvest." At that time the householder will tell the reapers to tie the weeds into bundles for fuel and to gather the wheat into his barns.

After recounting this parable, Jesus continues with stories about a mustard seed and leaven (13:31–33). God's reign is like the amazing contrast between the small mustard seed or leaven and the large shade tree or the abundant measures of leavened flour. Matthew's community knows that God's reign is small in its beginnings. But they trust that on the day of judgment the kingdom will be revealed to include both Jews and Gentiles. Matthew then concludes this part of the discourse with the comment that when Jesus speaks to the crowds in parables, he fulfills

the plan that God announced in the Hebrew scriptures
(13:34–35).

Inside the House (13:36–50)

Leaving the crowds at the lake, Jesus moves back into
the house where he continues to teach and explain to his
disciples the mysteries of the reign of God (13:36). First he
explains the story about the wheat and weeds (13:37–43).
Jesus says that until his second coming the kingdom will
include a mix of wheat and weeds—of good and evil. He
admonishes his disciples not to separate the good from the
evil. Instead, they are to wait patiently for the end time
when Jesus will return to make that judgment. Hearing
this interpretation, the faithful in Antioch reflect on the
mix of good and evil both within the community and
in their relations with the Pharisees at Jamnia and
with Rome.

Jesus then compares God's reign to men who find a
treasure in a field and a pearl of great price (13:44–46). In
his story, a poor farmer plows a field in which the rich
owner has buried his treasure to protect it against invasion
and revolt. When the poor man discovers the hidden treasure, he is overwhelmed by joy and immediately buys the
field. Similarly, the well-to-do merchant on the lookout for
precious pearls finds one of great price and sells all his
possessions to possess it. Matthew's community concludes
that they too must respond wholeheartedly to the treasure
and the pearl revealed in Jesus' words and actions, namely,
that God's reign is present and active in the world.

Lastly, Jesus tells his disciples a story about a net let
down into the sea (13:47–50). He explains that fishermen,
like Peter and Andrew, James and John (4:18–22), throw a

large dragnet into the sea. When the net is filled, the men pull it up onto the shore and sort out the fish, keeping the good ones and throwing away the bad ones. Jesus applies this parable to the end time, when God's angels will separate the evil from the righteous and throw the evil into a furnace of fire. Seeing the similarities to the story of the wheat and the weeds, the faithful at Antioch know that they must carry out their mission and leave all judgment to the Son of Man at the end of the age.

Finally, Jesus asks the disciples, "Have you understood all this?" The disciples' answer confirms that they have received the gift from God to understand the mysteries of the reign of God. Jesus then says, "Therefore every scribe who has been trained for the kingdom of heaven is like a householder who brings out of his treasure what is new and what is old" (13:52). In Matthew the evangelist, the community at Antioch sees this householder.

When Jesus has finished teaching in parables, he returns to his own people in Nazareth (13:53–58). As is his custom, he teaches them in the Jewish synagogue. At first his townspeople are fascinated. But questioning where he attained such wisdom, they are scandalized at his power. Jesus says: "A prophet is not without honor except in his own country and in his own house." Because his townspeople lack faith in his power, Jesus does not exercise his power to heal the sick in Nazareth. This event, which reminds Matthew's community that Jesus moved from Nazareth to Capernaum to begin his public ministry (4:12–17), echoes his harsh words against other cities in Galilee that did not repent and against this evil generation of Jews (11:20–24; 12:38–45). The response of his hometown also supports Jesus' words about his disciples being his true family (12:46–50).

Reflection Questions

- How do you react to Jesus' preaching, teaching, and healing? With whom do you most identify—Jesus' followers, the crowds, his enemies, the evil generation of Israel? Do you want to react differently?
- What do you like about the parables? What do you resist? Spend some time with your reactions.
- Let these stories tease you into thought about the mysteries of God's reign. How do you see these mysteries revealed in your family, in your neighborhood, at work, in the church?

Readings

For further discussion see M. Boucher, *The Parables.* Wilmington: Michael Glazier, 1981. J. Donahue, *The Gospel in Parable.* Philadelphia: Fortress Press, 1988. J. Lambrecht, *Once More Astonished.* New York: Crossroad, 1981.

For the earlier discussion of parables see C.H. Dodd, *The Parables of the Kingdom.* Glasgow: William Collins Sons, 1961. J. Jeremias, *The Parables of Jesus.* New York: Charles Scribner's Sons, 1972. D. Crossan, *In Parables.* San Francisco: Harper and Row, 1985.

For a detailed analysis of Matthew 13 see J.D. Kingsbury, *The Parables of Jesus in Matthew 13.* Atlanta: John Knox Press, 1969.

11

Jesus Forms the Disciples; Events Concerning Bread (14:1–16:12)

Matthew's story moves ahead once again with an event concerning John the Baptist. Herod Antipas, son of Herod the Great, says about Jesus: "This is John the Baptist, he has been raised from the dead; that is why these powers are at work in him." Then Matthew flashes back to tell how Herod finally had the imprisoned John killed. Although Herod "wanted to put him to death, he feared the people, because they held him to be a prophet" (14:5). Finally, Matthew relates the dramatic tale of how John was beheaded (14:1–12).

Matthew next narrates a series of events concerning bread in which Jesus teaches his followers while continuing to heal the crowds and debate with the Jewish religious authorities. At center stage Jesus forms his disciples. Jesus invites them to deepen their little faith and leads his followers to see, hear, and understand what his words and actions reveal. Matthew shapes these events into another well-ordered sequence:

First Series of Events
A 14:13–21   Feeding Five Thousand
B 14:22–36   Dismissing the Crowds; Crossing the Lake
C 15:1–20   Disputing with the Pharisees; Instructing the Disciples

Central Event
15:21–28 HEALING THE CANAANITE WOMAN'S
DAUGHTER

Second Series of Events
A′ 15:29–38 Feeding Four Thousand
B′ 15:39 Dismissing the Crowds; Crossing
the Lake
C′ 16:1–20 Disputing with the Pharisees;
Instructing the Disciples

First Series (14:13–15:20)

After hearing about John's death, Jesus withdraws
from the Lake of Tiberias to a more deserted place nearby
(14:13–21). Galilean crowds of Jews and Gentiles—those
who heard his parables—follow him to that place, where he
heals their sick. At evening the disciples ask Jesus to send
the crowd away from that lonely place, but Jesus tells them
to feed the people. The disciples object that they have
nothing more than five loaves and two fishes. Taking the
bread and fish, Jesus then "looked up to heaven, and
blessed, and broke and gave the loaves to the disciples, and
the disciples gave them to the crowds" (14:19). After the
crowds eat and are satisfied, the disciples pick up enough
bits and pieces to fill twelve baskets.

After dismissing the crowds of Jews and Gentiles,
Jesus commands his disciples to cross the lake without
him, goes up the mountain to pray, and in the early morning walks on the water through a storm to his disciples in
their boat (14:22–33). The disciples think he is a ghost and
are afraid. But Jesus assures them: "Take heart, it is I;
have no fear." Peter asks: "Lord, if it is you, bid me come to

you on the water." Jesus says: "Come!" Peter steps out of the boat and begins to walk on the water. But then he becomes frightened and begins to sink beneath the waves. Jesus catches him, saying: "O man of little faith, why did you doubt?" With Peter and Jesus back in the boat and with the storm subsided, the disciples all bow down before Jesus, saying: "Truly you are the Son of God" (14:33).

In the land of Gennesaret, that is, on the northwest shore of the lake, crowds again bring their sick to Jesus from all around. As many as touch the fringe of his garment are healed (14:34–36). Scribes and Pharisees then come from Jerusalem to test Jesus. Jesus counters with a question about why they value their traditions more than the commandment of God. He calls them hypocrites and cites the prophet Isaiah against his enemies (15:1–9).

Jesus then makes an enigmatic statement to the bystanders: "Hear and understand: not what goes into the mouth defiles a man, but what comes out of the mouth, this defiles a man" (15:20–21). When his followers tell Jesus that the Pharisees are offended, he advises them to ignore these "blind guides." When the disciples ask him for an explanation, he rebukes them: "Are you also still without understanding?" (15:16). Jesus then names the evil thoughts and actions that come out of the mouth and heart to truly defile a man or woman.

Canaanite Woman's Daughter (15:21–28)

Next Jesus goes further north to the border with the Phoenician cities of Tyre and Sidon. A Gentile woman from that area crosses the border to ask that he heal her daughter (15:21–28). Convinced that Jesus can heal her daughter, this suppliant woman acts on that conviction.

When Jesus' followers ask him to send her away, he tries to put her off: "I was sent only to the lost sheep of the house of Israel." But the woman persists: "Have mercy on me, O Lord, Son of David. My daughter is severely possessed by a demon. . . . Lord, help me. . . . Yes, Lord, yet even the dogs eat the crumbs that fall from their masters' table." Jesus commends this non-Israelite woman for her unshakable conviction about his power to heal her daughter: "O woman, great is your faith! Be it done for you as you desire" (15:28). Matthew relates that at that very moment the woman's daughter is healed in their home in Gentile territory.

Second Series (15:29–16:12)

Back at Lake Tiberias, the crowd of Jews and Gentiles again come to Jesus. Once again he heals their sick and multiplies bread and fish to feed them (15:29–38). Matthew presents the same actors—Jesus, the crowds, and the disciples—and the same actions as in the previous event (14:13–21). Again Jesus "took the seven loaves and the fish, and having given thanks he broke them and gave them to the disciples, and the disciples gave them to the crowds" (15:36). In this event, however, Jesus talks less to his followers and shows more compassion on the crowds, saying "I have compassion on the crowd, because they have been with me now three days, and have nothing to eat; and I am unwilling to send them away hungry, lest they faint on the way" (15:32). After the disciples distribute the bread and fish, the crowds eat and are satisfied, and the disciples collect seven baskets of bits and pieces.

Again Jesus dismisses the crowds and crosses the lake with his disciples (15:39). On the other side, Pharisees and Sadducees again test Jesus by challenging him to show them a sign from heaven (16:1–4). Jesus responds: "An evil and adulterous generation seeks for a sign but no sign shall be given to it except the sign of Jonah."

In the last event Jesus again makes an enigmatic statement about the leaven of the Pharisees (16:5–12). When his followers again fail to understand, he rebukes them: "O men of little faith, why do you discuss among yourselves the fact that you have no bread? Do you not yet perceive? Do you not remember the five loaves for the five thousand, and how many baskets you gathered? Or the seven loaves for the four thousand, and how many baskets you gathered? How is it that you fail to perceive that I did not speak about bread? Beware the leaven of the Pharisees and Sadducees." Matthew ends this section by stating that the disciples "understood that he did not tell them to beware of the leaven of bread, but of the teaching of the Pharisees and Sadducees" (16:12). Jesus has led his disciples from misunderstanding to understanding the deeper meaning that is hidden in these events concerning bread.

All the characters come on stage in these events. Jesus is at center stage with his followers. But John the Baptist, crowds of Jews and Gentiles, the suppliant Canaanite woman, and the Pharisees and Sadducees all make an appearance. When Matthew's community hears about John's death, they remember John and Jesus at the Jordan (3:1–17). They recall that Herod put John in prison (4:12–25) and that John sent word to Jesus through his disciples (11:1–19). Since John has paralleled Jesus, the faithful at Antioch anticipate that a similar death awaits the messiah.

In these events, Galilean Jews and Gentiles continue to bring their sick to Jesus to be healed and are satisfied with the bread and fish he multiplies. Matthew's community recalls earlier miracles of healing (8:1–9:34; 12:15–21). As they watch the Canaanite woman model faith in Jesus' power to heal, they think of other suppliants, especially the

Roman centurion (8:5–13), as well as the exorcism of two demoniacs in the non-Jewish territory of the Gadarenes (8:28–34). The Christians in Antioch relate these events to the mix of Jews and Gentiles and of men and women in their community.

Jesus continues to debate with the Pharisees and Sadducees, calling them "hypocrites," "blind guides," and "an evil and adulterous generation." Matthew's community hear echoes of similar words in the sermon on the mount (6:1–18), in Jesus' debates with the scribes and Pharisees (12:1–37), and in his condemnation of this evil generation (12:38–45). These events invite those in Antioch to wonder where this conflict will end and to think about their enemies—the Pharisees at Jamnia.

Above all, Jesus calls his followers to a deeper faith and understanding. The disciples often approach Jesus with comments or questions, and Jesus calls them "men of little faith" and rebukes them for their lack of understanding. In contrast, he commends the Canaanite woman for her great faith. The community at Antioch recalls that Jesus rebuked his disciples and calmed the storm at sea (8:18–27), that he thanked his Father for giving understanding to these little ones (11:25–26), and that he explained the parables because he wanted them to see, hear and understand the mysteries of the kingdom (13:1–52). These events invite the community to trace their own movement from misunderstanding to understanding, from little faith to deeper faith.

Central to these episodes are bread and water. Jesus twice multiplies bread and fish, telling his disciples to distribute this food to the crowds. Twice he crosses the lake to encounter his enemies. Twice he warns his disciples about the Pharisees and Sadducees. These events remind Matthew's listeners of God leading Israel out of slavery in Egypt, of Israel crossing the Red Sea into the desert, and of God feeding Israel with abundant manna-bread from heaven (Ex 14–19). The Jews and Gentiles in Matthew's community also see these events foreshadowing their sharing in a common eucharistic meal.

Reflection Questions

- Who are included in your Christian community? Who are excluded? Do you want your community to become more inclusive?
- Again, with whom are you in conflict? How do you manage the conflict? How can you manage it better?
- How do you—individuals and communities—move from misunderstanding to understanding what following Jesus means? How have you grown in faith?
- Recall how you celebrate your faith. What would make the celebration more meaningful?

Readings

J. Murphy-O'Connor. "The Structure of Matthew XIV–XVII," *Revue Biblique* 82 (1975) 360–384.

12

Journey to Jerusalem; Initiation into Paradox (16:13–20:34)

One of the most significant turning points in Matthew's story is the conversations at Caesarea Philippi (16:13–28). After Peter professes that Jesus is the Messiah and Son of God, Jesus names Peter the rock of his church and keeper of the keys to God's reign (16:13–20). When Jesus predicts that as Son of Man he must suffer, die, and be raised, the same Peter rebukes him, and Jesus reprimands Peter (16:21–23). Jesus then begins to instruct his disciples that they must take up their cross and follow him through suffering to glory (16:24–28).

Matthew the evangelist says that Jesus came to the neighborhood of Caesarea Philippi (16:13). Here begins the journey that Jesus takes with his followers through Capernaum along the Jordan valley to Jericho. This journey symbolizes initiation into the mystery of Jesus' suffering, death, and resurrection and its implications for his disciples. The disciples continually fail to see the paradox that the way to glory is through suffering, but two blind men at Jericho receive their physical sight and follow Jesus to watch the mystery unfold (20:29–34). The journey ends with Jesus entering Jerusalem and the temple (21:1–17). Matthew invites his community into this mystery.

When Jesus asks his disciples what others say about him, they respond: "Some say John the Baptist, others say Elijah, and others Jeremiah or one of the prophets" (16:14). Matthew's listeners know that John the Baptist was Elijah, and they recall Herod's statement that Jesus is the Baptist returned from the dead (14:1–2). Jeremiah was killed by his own people as he predicted the destruction of Jerusalem. Jesus then challenges his disciples: "But who do you say that I am?" (16:15). He asks his closest followers what they have come to know about him after seeing his actions and hearing his words throughout Galilee. Peter speaks for himself and for the others when he says, "You are the Christ, the Son of the living God" (16:16). His words echo what all the disciples said when Jesus walked to them on the water (14:33). Matthew's community uses the same words to profess their faith in Jesus.

Jesus responds by giving Peter a new title and a special role (16:17–19). Peter's declaration could only be inspired by a revelation from the Father, so Jesus now changes his name from Simon to Peter, "the rock." His new name indicates that he is to be the firm, bedrock foundation on which Jesus will build his holy assembly, the true Israel, his church. Jesus prophesies that evil powers, even death and hell, will not destroy that community. Next, Jesus gives Peter the keys of the kingdom of heaven, symbols of the power that a majordomo has to control who enters into the presence of his master. Peter is to allow or refuse entrance to those who come to the messiah's palace (see Is 22:22). Finally, Jesus gives Peter power to bind and loose, that is, to decide what practices and activities are consistent with his teaching. What Peter decides on earth, God will confirm in heaven. The community at Antioch reflects on all that Peter did until his martyrdom under Nero.

After Jesus commands the disciples to tell no one that he is the messiah, he begins to show them "that he must go to Jerusalem and suffer many things from the elders and chief priests and scribes, and be killed, and on the third day be raised" (16:21). His prediction shocks and startles his followers since, like their fellow Jews, they long for a messiah who will free them from Roman domination and reinstate Israel to its former glory as a prosperous and prominent nation under God. Jesus violates those expectations by beginning to reveal the paradoxical mystery that his mission from God is to be Israel's messiah through suffering and death and resurrection.

Peter reacts to Jesus' prediction with the vehement cry, "God forbid, Lord! This shall never happen to you!" (16:22). Jesus rebukes Peter: "Get behind me, Satan! You are a hindrance to me; for you are not on the side of God, but of men" (16:23). Thus Peter the rock becomes Peter the stumbling block because he does not understand that Jesus must be the suffering Son of Man. As Satan tempted Jesus in the desert, so Peter now tries to turn Jesus away from the mysterious journey through suffering to glory that his Father has chosen to be his messianic mission.

Jesus next instructs his disciples that they must follow him on that same journey (16:24–28). His followers must deny themselves and take up their cross. They must lose their life to save it, so that they might imitate their master. If they let the paradox in Jesus' suffering, death, and resurrection shape their lives, they will be rewarded when he returns in glory as the triumphant Son of Man. Matthew's community asks how this mystery is found in their own experience.

At Caesarea Philippi Jesus has *predicted* that he must suffer, die, and rise again, Peter has *misunderstood* his prediction, and Jesus has *instructed* his disciples. Matthew repeats these activities twice on the way to Jerusalem:

Jesus predicts	17:22–23b	20:17–19
Disciples misunderstand	17:23c	20:20–23
Jesus instructs	17:24–18:35	20:24–28

The evangelist arranges other events around this prediction/misunderstanding/instruction pattern:

A   First Pattern (16:21–28)
    B   Other Events: transfiguration, the epileptic boy (17:1–21)
A′   Second Pattern (17:22–18:35)
    B′   Other Events: marriage, children, riches (19:1–20:16)
A″   Third Pattern (20:17–28)
Conclusion: Two Blind Men at Jericho (20:29–34)

Matthew's community experiences the inner movement into paradox that dominates Jesus' outward journey to Jerusalem. Tension between Jesus' predictions and the disciples' misunderstanding creates suspense. They wonder if the events that Jesus predicts will actually take place and if his disciples will ever understand. Only at the end of the story do they find answers to these questions.

Jesus next takes Peter, James, and John up a mountain to catch a glimpse of his glory as they see him transfigured (17:1–13). His radiant face and white garments reveal that he belongs in the world of heavenly light. During this mysterious interlude, Jesus speaks with Moses and Elijah. (Both received a revelation from God on Mount Sinai, both were believed to have been taken up to heaven without dying, and both were expected to return in the end-time.) In speaking with them, Jesus inaugurates that end-time and fulfills the Hebrew scriptures.

Peter, always impetuous, wants to build tents for Jesus, Moses, and Elijah. But while he speaks, a radiant cloud descends from above to envelop all of them. From the cloud that both reveals and hides God's presence, a voice is heard: "This is my beloved Son, with whom I am well pleased; listen to him" (17:5). Thus, Jesus is revealed to be the servant of God his Father. His followers are to listen to him predict his death and resurrection and heed his instructions. When Peter, James, and John fall on their face with holy fear, Jesus reassures them: "Rise, and have no fear" (17:7). Matthew's community in Antioch remembers the similar revelation at Jesus' baptism (3:13–17).

Having initiated them into his ultimate triumph, Jesus tells Peter, James, and John to keep secret what they have seen until after his death and resurrection. The three men then raise a question about Elijah (17:10–13). They ask how Jesus can be the messiah and introduce the end-time when Elijah has not returned. Jesus points out that John the Baptist was Elijah, that Israel did not recognize him as Elijah, and that Herod killed him because of that blindness. Finally, Jesus indicates that what happened to John foreshadows what will happen to him in Jerusalem. The faithful at Antioch identify with the disciples who seem to understand about John but do not yet understand about Jesus.

Second Pattern (17:22–18:35)

At the center of this section is the second prediction/ misunderstanding/instruction pattern (17:22–18:35). Within it Jesus instructs his followers about how they are to live the paradox of his death and resurrection in community. Matthew arranges Jesus' words in another orderly pattern, so that his community might let them interact with their experience:

Prediction–Misunderstanding (17:22–23)

Instructions:
A   Peter: Payment of the Half-Shekel Tax
    (17:24–27)
B   Disciples:
    General Norm: True Greatness in the
                      Kingdom of Heaven
                      (18:1–4)

       Specific Situations:
        a   The Evil of Scandal (18:5–9)
        b   The Care of Sheep Going Astray
           (18:10–14)
        a'   Reconciling a Brother (18:15–20)
A'   Peter: Forgiveness in the Kingdom of
    Heaven (18:21–35).

Again Jesus predicts his death and resurrection, and again his followers misunderstand (17:22–23). Jesus then talks to Peter about paying the half-shekel tax (17:24–27), and he later talks with Peter about unlimited forgiveness (18:21–35). At the center of this fourth discourse, Jesus teaches the disciples about true greatness in the reign of God (18:1–4). He shows them the evil of scandal, he demonstrates with a story the value of one community member who has gone astray, and he explains how they must try to reconcile a brother who has sinned (18:5–20).

First, Jesus responds when the disciples ask: "Who is the greatest in the kingdom of heaven?" (18:1–4). Jesus summons a child, who is powerless to defend himself and relies totally on others for life and sustenance. Jesus assures his followers that true greatness in the kingdom means paradoxically that they must become like children —they must recognize their littleness and trust their Father in heaven. Like children, they must accept their vulnerability with honest humor, face their present suffering with humility, and let their imaginations create a future with new possibilities. Jesus promises that those who adopt the attitudes of children will both enter and be great in the kingdom of heaven. The adult Christians at Antioch ponder what being children might mean.

Then Jesus continues his discourse by saying that whoever receives such a childlike disciple receives Jesus, since he is identified with that disciple. But someone may scandalize one of these little ones, someone may cause a little one to fall from faith through sin. Jesus states that drowning would be better for such a member than suffering eternal damnation. Next, Jesus explains that scandal within the community may be included in the tribulations that must come before the end-time. Nevertheless, he laments for the disciple whose selfishness, lust, or power causes the scandal. Losing hand or foot or eye is better than the damnation that will come to those who weaken the faith of little ones. Hearing these words, the members of Matthew's community reflect on their own mutual hatred and betrayal.

Instead of causing scandal, Jesus declares that the disciples are to care for the little ones so that they do not get lost (18:10–14). He assures his listeners that angels watch over these children and plead with their Father in heaven. Next, he tells a story in which God is like a shepherd who is concerned for his flock. Jesus concludes that true followers will mirror God's concern by taking special care of weaker members in the community. Like a shepherd, they will risk leaving the ninety-nine other sheep to search for the one that has wandered away from the flock. When they find it, they will know more joy than if they had remained to keep the ninety-nine safe and sound.

Jesus next speaks more specifically about the case of a brother who wanders away through sin (18:15–20). A true disciple, he notes, will show the same zeal as the shepherd in trying to win back the sinner to the community. With loving correction, a true disciple will approach his brother privately so as to protect his honor. If that effort fails, he will try again with two witnesses to support his intervention. If that fails, he will bring the case to the assembled community. Should his brother still refuse to return, he is to be considered an outsider, like the pagans who do not belong to God's people or the hated tax collectors who exploit their fellow Jews.

Finally, Jesus affirms that God will ratify the community's final decision, since it is based on the assembly's power to "bind" and "loose," that is, to admit or exclude persons from membership. Jesus says that after the community members have reached a consensus in prayer, God will accept that decision as his own, since Jesus himself is with two or three who are gathered to pray in his name (18:18–20). Matthew tells his community that, gathered in Jesus' name, his followers experience Jesus both as Emmanuel—God-with-us (1:23)—and as their risen Lord, who is with them to the end of the age (28:20). Hearing these words, the faithful at Antioch reflect on how they treat those who have wandered away from their community.

In the final exchange, Jesus teaches Peter about forgiveness (18:21–35). Peter asks: "Lord, how often shall my brother sin against me, and I forgive him? As many as seven times?" Jesus answers: "I do not say to you seven times, but seventy times seven." Paradoxically, true disciples are to forgive their fellow disciples without bounds.

In contrast, Jesus then tells a story about a servant who owes his king a billion dollars from the taxes he has collected. When the debtor begs time to pay the deficit, the king generously forgives him by wiping out the debt and freeing his servant from all obligation. On his way home, however, when that same servant meets another servant who owes him a day's wages, he demands immediate payment. His fellow servant appeals for time, but the unforgiving servant sends him to prison until he pays the debt in full. Other servants, shocked at his lack of compassion, report his conduct to the king. The king then summons his unforgiving servant, denounces his actions, and hands him over to the torturers for punishment until his enormous debt is paid. Jesus concludes with the moral to this story: "So also my heavenly Father will do to every one of you, if you do not forgive your brother from your heart" (18:35). Hearing this, Matthew's community recalls Jesus' earlier words about prayer and forgiveness (6:7–15) and reflects on their own practice of mutual forgiveness.

As the journey continues, Jesus teaches how the paradox of his suffering, death, and resurrection applies to remarriage, to children, and to riches in the reign of God (19:1–30). About marriage, Jesus says: "Whoever divorces his wife, except for unchastity, and marries another, commits adultery. . . . There are eunuchs who have made themselves eunuchs for the sake of the kingdom of heaven." Here, the faithful at Antioch remember Jesus' earlier teaching about divorce (5:31–32) and discuss their own attitude toward marriage and divorce.

About children, Jesus tells his disciples: "Let the children come to me, and do not hinder them; for to such belongs the kingdom of heaven." About riches, Jesus states: "Every one who has left houses or brothers or sisters or father or mother or children or lands, for my name's sake, will receive a hundredfold, and inherit eternal life. But many that are first will be last, and the last first." Jesus then tells a story about a vineyard owner who at the end of the day pays all his workers the same wages. He concludes: "So the last will be first, and the first last." These words remind Matthew's community of the beatitudes (5:3–12) and the instructions about true greatness in the kingdom (18:1–4).

Third Pattern (20:17–28)

As Jesus draws closer to Jerusalem his predictions are more detailed; his disciples' seem more ambitious; and Jesus' instructions reach their climax (20:17–28). After the mother of James and John asks that her sons might sit at Jesus' side in his glory, Jesus teaches his disciples: "You know that the rulers of the Gentiles lord it over them, and their great men exercise authority over them. It shall not be so among you; but whoever would be great among you must be your servant, and whoever would be first among you must be your slave; even as the Son of man came not to be served but to serve, and to give his life as a ransom for many" (20:25–28). The community at Antioch thus learns that following Jesus means viewing reality as ultimately paradoxical and mysterious. It means becoming great by serving others, being first by being slave of all. Jesus' followers are to imitate their master who came to serve others by passing through suffering and death to the glory of resurrection.

As Jesus and his followers leave Jericho, he gives sight to two blind men (20:29–34). Like other suppliants, these blind men are convinced that Jesus can heal them. They shout: "Have mercy on us, Son of David!" When Jesus calls out to them and heals them, the two men follow him up the road toward Jerusalem. Now able to use their eyes, they join his followers and the crowds to see and hear all that awaits Jesus in the city of David. Witnessing this cure, Matthew's listeners recall how Jesus called four fishermen and a tax collector, as well as how he healed the sick throughout Galilee. The Antioch community prays that they, like Jesus' followers, may move from blindness to sight, from little faith to deeper faith, from misunderstanding to understanding the paradox and mystery revealed in this journey to Jerusalem.

Reflection Questions

- What do you like about this section? What do you resist? Spend time with your reactions to see where they lead.
- What surfaces in you when you hear the word *paradox?* What did others tell you about paradox? What has your experience told you?
- Do you identify with Peter and the disciples, with the blind men at Jericho?
- Does scandal happen in your family or church, at work or in your neighborhood? How do you care for

those little ones who have wandered into destructive conflicts, violence, or addictions?
- Have you ever found your life by losing it, become great by serving others? Do you know people who model this paradox?

Readings

R.E. Brown, et al., "Peter in the Gospel of Matthew," in *Peter in the New Testament*. Mahwah: Paulist Press, 1973, pages 75–107.

W.G. Thompson, *Matthew's Advice to a Divided Community—Mt 17:22–18:35*. Rome: Biblical Institute Press, 1970.

13

Jesus and the Temple in Jerusalem; Predicting the End of the Age (21:1–23:39)

Matthew's story takes a significant turn when Jesus enters Jerusalem and the temple (21:1–17). A day of triumph! After driving out the buyers and sellers, Jesus welcomes and heals the blind and the lame who by law are not allowed into the temple area. Crowds from Galilee call Jesus "Son of David" and "the prophet Jesus from Nazareth of Galilee." In the temple, children cry, "Hosanna to the Son of David!" But Jesus' enemies, the Jewish chief priests and scribes, who are responsible for keeping order, confront Jesus with their indignant complaint. Jesus' success surprises Matthew's listeners. They recall similar healings and reactions in Galilee (8:1–9:34; 12:15–32) and wonder whether Jesus is indeed greater than the temple (12:6).

The temple in Jerusalem was the civic, cultural, and economic center of Judaism, as well as the sacred place where the Jews gathered to worship their God. Herod began to build a new temple in A.D. 19. He meant this edifice to be a gift to the Jews that might lessen their hostility toward him because he was an Idumean, a foreigner. His religion was more heathen than Jewish. The temple was completed in A.D. 29. But the work of decoration continued until A.D. 64. Six years later the Romans

116

destroyed that temple when they plundered Jerusalem (A.D. 70).

The temple grounds included several courts. Anyone could enter the large outer court of the Gentiles, but only Jews were permitted to enter the interior courts. Raised five steps above the court of the Gentiles was the court of the women with its alms boxes for contributions to the temple worship. Another five steps higher was the court where Jewish men stood during the incense offerings. Priests passed from there to the holy court to offer sacrifice according to the Jewish law.

Inside the temple stood the holy place with the altar of incense, the table of shewbread, and the seven-branched lampstand. A veil hid from view the most holy place, the holy of holies, an empty space totally dark, where the Jews believed the God of Israel to be present to the chosen people. The high priest entered that most sacred place only once a year—on the Day of Atonement.

Matthew presents Jesus' activities on his second day in Jerusalem. He confronts his enemies in the temple (21:18–23:39); across from the temple, he teaches his disciples about the end of the age (24:1–25:46). Fifteen years after Rome destroyed the temple (A.D. 70), the community in Antioch relates Jesus' words and actions to their conflicts with the Pharisees at Jamnia and to their hopes for the future.

On his way to Jerusalem Jesus curses the fig tree for not bearing fruit. This action anticipates how his enemies will also be judged. He also urges his followers to deepen their weak faith through prayer, to have faith without doubt (21:18–22).

Back in the temple, the Jewish religious authorities confront Jesus. First, the chief priests and elders, those responsible for worship in the temple, ask Jesus about his authority (21:23–27). Later, the Sadducees question Jesus about the resurrection of the dead (22:23–33). But his principal enemies continue to be the Pharisees who confronted him in Galilee (12:1–37). Now in the temple, the same Pharisees begin to orchestrate the opposition against Jesus. First, they take counsel to trap Jesus in a question about paying taxes to Rome (22:15–22). Next, they send one of their lawyers to ask him about the greatest commandment in the Jewish law (22:34–40). Finally, when the Pharisees again take counsel against Jesus, he tests them with a question about David's son and reduces them to silence (22:41–46). Although all the Jewish authorities challenge Jesus, the Pharisees remain his chief opponents. In contrast, the Jewish crowds remain astonished at his teaching (22:33). Matthew's community associates these Pharisees with their adversaries in post-war Judaism.

These conflict-stories follow a pattern. They have four elements: *setting—test—response—reactions.*

	Setting	Test	Response	Reactions
In Galilee:				
Plucking Grain	12:1	2	3–8	
Healing on the Sabbath	12:9–10a	10b	11–13	14
In the Temple:				
Jesus Authority	21:23a	23b	24–27	
Paying Taxes to Caesar	22:15–16a	16b–17	18–21	22
The Resurrection	22:23	24–28	29–32	33
The Great Commandment	22:34–35	36	37–40	

The conflicts between Jesus and his enemies dramatize the deeper struggle between Satan and Jesus, the hidden apocalyptic battle between the power of evil and the reign of God. Jesus confronts evil at work in his enemies, who test him with difficult questions. With counter-questions and disarming dialogue, Jesus wins every debate, revealing once again that the reign of God is more powerful than the forces of evil. In the final confrontation, Jesus takes the initiative. He asks the Pharisees about David's son and completes his victory by reducing them to silence: "And no one was able to answer him a word, nor from that day did anyone dare to ask him any more questions" (22:46). Recalling that Jesus' battle with evil began when he confronted Satan in the desert (4:1–11) and was at work in his miracles in Galilee (8:1–9:35), Matthew's community wonders if their struggles with the Pharisees at Jamnia are part of the same apocalyptic conflict.

Between conflicts, Jesus tells his enemies three parables about God's judgment on official Israel (21:28–22:14). In the first story, a son does his father's will after repenting of earlier rebellion, but a second son renders only lip-service to God without doing God's will. Jesus then says that tax collectors and harlots—religious outcasts in official Judaism—repented because of John the Baptist's preaching. However, the self-satisfied leaders of Israel, feeling no need to repent, failed to do what God wanted.

Next, Jesus tells about a vineyard owner and his wicked vinedressers. The vineyard is God's reign revealed in the Hebrew scriptures. God is the owner; God's servants are the prophets of Israel; God's Son is Jesus. The murderous vinedressers are the people of Israel, especially their religious leaders. The others to whom the vineyard will be given are outcasts like the blind and the lame, the harlots and tax collectors, and the Gentiles. Israel and its leaders condemn themselves when they kill both the prophets and God's own Son. Jesus concludes the parable with these words: "Therefore I tell you, the kingdom of God will be taken away from you and given to a nation producing the fruits of it" (21:43). His enemies, the chief priests and Pharisees, know that Jesus speaks about them. But they dare not arrest him because the crowds consider him a prophet.

Finally, Jesus describes a wedding feast. In this third

story, the invited guests are the Jews to whom the reign of
God was first revealed. When they murder the king's servants, he sends his army to retaliate and burn their city.
The new guests who fill the wedding hall are again the
outcasts, both good and bad. One man without a wedding
garment is cast into external darkness. He may have repented but he has not lived according to the attitudes and
values of God's reign. Hearing these stories, the Christians
in Antioch learn why Gentiles continue to join their community and why the Pharisees at Jamnia continue to be
their enemies. They also see that they are not to be complacent because they replace the false Israel. In the end
they may be excluded. So their lives must bear the fruits of
repentance.

Scribes and Pharisees (23:1–36)

Jesus' tension with his enemies in the temple ends
with dramatic words about the scribes and the Pharisees.
He first instructs his disciples and the crowds about their
life-style (23:1–12). He points out that the scribes and the
Pharisees preach but do not practice. With their binding
interpretations, they put heavy burdens on the common
people of Israel and do not lift a finger to help their people
observe the Jewish law. Also, they do all their deeds to be
seen by men. In contrast, Jesus' followers will not be called
"rabbi" or "master" because Jesus is their only teacher and
their Christ. Nor are they to call anyone "father" because
their Father is in heaven. Instead, they are to live out the
paradox that Jesus has been teaching. He sums up the
mystery by insisting, "He who is greatest among you shall
be your servant; whoever exalts himself will be humbled,
and whoever humbles himself will be exalted" (23:11–12).
Jesus next balances the beatitudes with seven harsh

woes against the scribes and the Pharisees (23:13–36). "Woe" expresses Jesus' sadness that his enemies are already dead within. He threatens eternal punishment because they pride themselves on their own achievements. He takes them to task for hindering entrance to God's reign, for insisting that Gentile converts submit to the Jewish law, for arguing speciously about oaths, for obliging the people to tithe, for not cleaning the inside of a cup while whitewashing tombs, and, finally, for killing the prophets, God's own servants.

Jesus ends with an emotional lament for Jerusalem (23:37–39). Jesus cries that the holy city has been an evil city, because in it the prophets have been rejected and murdered. God often protected Israel with a mother's love and concern, and now Jesus longs to protect Jerusalem and its temple with the same mother's care and compassion. He mourns that as Israel rejected God's prophets, so she now rejects God's Son, their own messiah. Because Jerusalem has missed its chance for salvation, the house of God—the temple—will be abandoned. He predicts that the city will not see its messiah again until he returns not on a donkey but on the clouds of heaven as the triumphant Son of Man.

As the Christians in Antioch reflect on Jesus' words about the scribes and the Pharisees, they recall that before the fall of Jerusalem to the Babylonians (587 B.C.), Jeremiah the prophet battled his enemies, warned them about impending disaster, and lamented the loss of both city and temple. His anguish was that God called him to condemn those whom he loved. Compassion for both God and Israel overwhelmed Jeremiah. As he stood before God, Jeremiah pleaded for his people. Standing before his recalcitrant people, he pleaded for God. Declaring the Babylonian threat to be God's judgment on Jerusalem, Jeremiah challenged his people to face the loss of their king and temple and to be open to God's leading them into exile.

When Jesus refers to the destruction of Jerusalem and the temple, Matthew's community is reminded of Jeremiah (7:1–34; 19:1–15; 26:1–19). They recall that at Caesarea Philippi the disciples mentioned "Jeremiah or one of the prophets" (16:14) and that Jesus explicitly named Jerusalem in his first prediction about his suffering and death (16:21). When Jesus enters the holy city, all of Jerusalem is disturbed because the crowds announce that he is "the prophet Jesus from Nazareth in Galilee" (21:10–11). Now, Jesus follows his sad lament for the holy city with predictions about the destruction of the temple and the end of the age. The Christian Jews and Gentiles in Antioch know that Jesus speaks the truth about Jerusalem.

Reflection Questions

- What did you like about these events? What did you fight? Spend time with your positive and negative reactions.
- What is your attitude toward anger and conflict?
- Why is our culture so fascinated with violence on film and television? Can Christians be non-violent?
- Do you find the apocalyptic struggle between good and evil at work in your personal life, in your relationships to family, work, and church, and in our society?

14

Jesus and the Temple in Jerusalem; Predicting the End of the Age (24:1–25:46)

Next, Matthew presents Jesus' discourse to his disciples about the end of the age (24:1–25:46). As Jesus leaves the temple area, his followers point to the buildings, and Jesus predicts their destruction: "There will not be left here one stone upon another that will not be thrown down" (24:2). Across the Kedron Valley on the Mount of Olives where they sit facing the temple, Jesus' disciples ask, "Tell us, when will this be, and what will be the sign of your coming and of the close of the age?" (24:3). Jesus teaches them about both the destruction of the temple and the end of the age (24:4–25:46).

Matthew has carefully arranged this last of the five discourses according to the following plan:

> *Phases of the Future (24:4–35)*
>   Not Yet the End (24:4–14)
>   Great Tribulation/Second Coming (24:15–31)
>   Assurance: Coming Soon (24:32–35)
> *Exhortation to Vigilance (24:36–25:30)*
>   Unknown Time (24:36–44)
>   Parable: Faithful and Unfaithful Servants (24:45–51)

123

Parable: Prudent and Foolish Bridesmaids
(25:1–13)
Parable: Talents (25:14–30)
Judgment of All Nations (25:31–46)

Jesus begins by describing what must happen to his disciples before the end of the age (24:4–14). They will see nation rising against nation, kingdom against kingdom; they will know famine and earthquake. Jesus says that these events will only begin the intense tribulation that the disciples must endure before the end (24:8). Hearing these predictions, Matthew's community thinks about the unsuccessful Jewish revolt against Rome (A.D. 66–70).

Next, Jesus says that all nations—Jews and Gentiles—will hate the disciples, deliver them up to tribulation, and put them to death because they believe him to be the messiah. The faithful in Antioch recall Nero who put Peter and Paul to death in Rome (A.D. 67–68) and the Pharisees at Jamnia who ban their Christian members from the Jewish synagogues.

Jesus explains how these external events will trigger internal dissension. He says: "And then many will fall away, and betray one another, and hate one another. And many false prophets will arise and lead many astray. And because wickedness is multiplied, most men's love will grow cold. But he who endures to the end will be saved" (24:10–12). Matthew's Christians reflect on how well Jesus has named their present tensions and recall the commandment to love God and neighbor (22:34–40).

Finally, Jesus describes the disciples' mission. He says, "This gospel of the kingdom will be preached throughout the whole world, as a testimony to all nations; and then the end will come" (24:14). He predicts that the end of the age will not come until the disciples have completed their mission to all nations. The Jews and Gentiles in Matthew's community hear in these words their mission to the entire world.

Continuing to describe the future, Jesus predicts a time of struggle in Judea (24:15–28). He states that enemies will violate the temple and that false prophets and false Christs will lead many of his followers astray. After that tribulation, God will act to establish his reign over the earth. Jesus describes the cosmic events that will announce his return as the triumphant Son of Man. He says: "Then will appear the sign of the Son of Man in heaven, and then all the tribes of the earth will mourn, and they will see the Son of Man coming on the clouds of heaven with power and great glory" (24:30). Jesus then assures his followers that his second coming is near (24:32–35). Matthew invites his community to keep an eye on this triumphant return of their risen Lord.

Vigilance (24:36–25:30)

Next, Jesus exhorts his followers to watch for his coming (24:36–25:30). Repeatedly he urges them to be alert because they cannot know the exact day and hour: "But of that day and hour no one knows, not even the angels of heaven, nor the Son, but the Father only" (24:36). "Watch, therefore, for you do not know on what day your Lord is coming" (24:42). "Therefore you also must be ready; for the Son of Man is coming at an hour you do not expect" (24:44). "The master of that servant will come on a day when he does not expect him and at an hour he does not know" (24:50).

Then in three parables, Jesus instructs his followers to keep their eye on his sudden, unexpected return (24:45–25:30). He tells the disciples stories about a master surprising his servants, about a bridegroom coming home at night to celebrate his wedding feast, and about a landowner asking an account of his stewards. Jesus wants his followers to imitate the faithful servants and the wise bridesmaids by being alert and by staying awake as they carry out their mission to the nations.

In each of these parables Jesus describes a *separation or division,* a *coming, rewards* and *punishments,* and a *criterion for judgment.* In the first story, the master separates his faithful servants from the unfaithful servants, when he surprises them with a return visit. He banishes the unfaithful servants into external darkness, because they have failed to do what their master wanted (24:43–51).

In the second parable, a bridegroom comes home late at night for his wedding feast (25:1–13). Then the wise bridesmaids enter the house to share in the celebration because they are prepared to greet him with their lamps trimmed. In contrast, the foolish bridesmaids do not partake in the festivities. Jesus makes his lesson clear by saying, "Watch, therefore, for you know neither the day nor the hour" (25:13).

Next, Jesus tells a story about a landowner who entrusts his property to three stewards (25:14–30). He gives them one, two, and five talents. The owner goes away; he later returns to settle accounts (25:14–30). Because they doubled their talents, he gives greater responsibility to two of his servants and invites them to share his joy. In contrast, the landowner punishes the steward who buried his one talent. He casts that servant into outer darkness because he feared his master and thought him to be a hard and cruel man.

Hearing these stories, Matthew's community reflects on how they might be ready for their master's return. They recall earlier stories about the wheat and the weeds and about the fish net cast into the sea (13:24–50). Jew and Gentile members talk about the roles they are to play in the mission to all nations. When Jesus returns, he will not judge them according to their abilities but according to how well they carried out their tasks with love and respect for one another.

Jesus ends this final discourse by describing the judgment of the nations to whom he sends his followers (25:31–46). When he returns as the triumphant Son of Man, Jesus will separate the nations into sheep and goats. He will invite the sheep to possess the kingdom of heaven; he will condemn the goats to eternal fire. Both sheep and goats will be surprised. Then Jesus will explain the criterion for judgment: how well or ill the nations treated the least of his brethren—the disciples who announced to them the gospel of God's reign. Jesus declares that he will reward or punish Jews and Gentiles according to whether or not they gave these missionaries food and drink, clothed and sheltered them, and visited them when sick or in prison. Without the nations knowing it, they encountered Jesus himself in these little ones because he sent them to announce the good news about God.

With this last discourse, Matthew's community looks beyond their present struggles to the ultimate triumph of God's reign. John the Baptist announced that reign; the words and actions of Jesus of Nazareth reveal it. Matthew wants his community to keep their eyes on the vision that Jesus gives of the future. At the end of the age, God's power will win over evil, God's love over hatred, God's truth over falsehood, God's life over death. To receive God's reign, the disciples must take its vision seriously, live according to its values, and take an active part in its mission. When Jesus returns at the end of the age, he will ask his followers— men and women, Jews and Gentiles—to give an account. He will reward or punish them according to how well they lived their commitment to God's reign; he will also judge the nations. After that final judgment, God will reign forever over all the world.

Reflection Questions

- What did you like about this discourse? What did you resist? What are your images of the future?
- Have you experienced tribulation in your family, among your friends, in your church or city? Was the outcome positive or negative?
- How would you retell Jesus' parables about the end of the age? Would they include a final judgment with rewards and punishments?
- How does your vision of the future influence your life in the present?

Reading

For an excellent treatment of the eschatological discourse, see J. Lambrecht, "The Parousia Discourse: Composition and Content in Mt 24–25," in *L'Evangile selon Matthieu: Redaction et Theologie.* Gembloux, Belgium: Editions J. Duculot, 1972, pages 243–262.

15

Passover Meal, Passion, Death, and Resurrection (26:1–27:31)

Matthew's story of Jesus' passion, death, and resurrection is a forceful drama. Moving rapidly from event to event, the evangelist describes the drama in sober, controlled language. As a prelude, Jesus again predicts his passion, his enemies concoct their death plot, a woman anoints his body for burial, and Judas contracts with Jesus' enemies to betray his master (26:1–16). Next, Jesus eats the Passover meal with his followers (26:17–35) and prays to his Father in Gethsemane (26:36–46). Several events then occur in quick succession: Jesus' arrest in the garden (26:47–56), the Jewish trial and Peter's denial (26:57–75), Judas' death and the Roman trial (27:1–31), Jesus' crucifixion and death (27:32–56), Jesus' burial and the setting of the Jewish guards (27:57–66), the women and Jesus at the empty tomb (28:1–10), and the bribing of the guards (28:11–15). Matthew's story ends in Galilee where Jesus appears to his eleven disciples to send them on a mission to all nations (28:16–20).

Matthew offers us a continuous story that is fast-moving yet deliberate, dramatic yet well ordered. Following the movement from place to place, from time to time, from event to event is easy—much easier than in the rest of the story. Transitional verses move us from one event

into the next: into the preliminaries (26:1–2), into the
Passover meal (26:17–19), into the garden (26:30,36), into
the Jewish trial (26:57–58), into the Roman trial (27:1–2),
into the crucifixion and death (27:31), into the request for
guards (27:62), into the discovery of the empty tomb (28:1),
into the bribing of the guards (28:11), and into the commission in Galilee (28:16). Within events, Matthew carefully notes the passage of time, as well as the movement
from place to place: within the preliminaries (26:3,6,14);
within the Passover meal (26:20–26); within Jesus' prayer
in the garden (26:37,46–47); within the Jewish trial
(26:59,69); within the Roman trial (27:3,11,15–17,24);
within the crucifixion (27:32–33,45,57). Matthew's community cherishes the evangelist's story about Jesus' last days
on earth.

Prediction–Plot–Anointing–Betrayal (26:1–16)

A solemn beginning! A new cast of characters! With
his usual formula, Matthew notes that Jesus finishes all his
teaching with his discourse on the end of the age and that
Jesus again predicts his death, echoing the predictions that
he made on the journey from Caesarea Philippi to Jerusalem (16:21; 17:22; 20:18–19). Next, the Jewish Sanhedrin
—the chief priests and elders of the people—gather at the
house of Caiaphas, the high priest, to plot how to arrest
and kill Jesus. The faithful in Antioch note that these
Jewish officials continue the intense conflict between
Jesus and the Pharisees (12:1–14; 21:18–23:39).

Outside Jerusalem, Jesus lodges in Bethany. Here an
unnamed woman anoints his body. When his disciples
protest, Jesus interprets her action as preparing his body
for burial. With other women she will witness his death on

the cross, see where he is buried, return to the tomb to find it empty, meet the risen Jesus, and carry news of his resurrection to the other disciples (27:55–56; 27:61; 28:1–11). In Jerusalem, meanwhile, Judas makes an agreement with the chief priests to betray Jesus for thirty pieces of silver. Judas' decision will lead to Jesus' arrest in the garden (26:47–56), Judas' tragic death (27:3–10), and Jesus' crucifixion (27:32–56). As the stage is set and the characters are introduced, Matthew's community senses how the story will unfold and recalls the infancy narrative (2:1–23).

Passover Meal (26:17–35)

After Jesus tells his disciples to prepare the Passover meal, they carry out his instructions. With its rich memories of Israel's exodus from Egypt, the Passover provides the larger landscape for understanding the deeper, hidden meaning of the events about to happen to Jesus. A new Passover for the true Israel!

At the ritual meal, Jesus predicts that one of his disciples will betray him. Calling him "Lord," the disciples question who among them would perform such an act. Jesus narrows the man to Judas, who then calls him "Rabbi." Jesus responds by saying that his death is more than an accident or a tragedy resulting from Judas' betrayal. He goes to his death as part of the deeply mysterious and paradoxical plan that his Father has chosen to save the world.

Later in the meal Jesus takes bread, blesses it, breaks it, and distributes it to the disciples for them to eat. He also blesses and distributes the cup. Matthew's community recalls how Jesus fed both the Jewish and the Gentile crowds (14:13–21; 15:29–39). Here Jesus links those feedings and this meal to his imminent death. He says that the bread that he breaks is his body which will be broken, crucified, buried, and raised. Then Jesus offers his followers the cup that contains his blood which will be poured out and restored. In eating bread and drinking wine with his followers at this Passover meal, Jesus creates a bond with them that completes God's covenant with Israel at Sinai. He promises that his followers will drink wine again in their Father's kingdom at the end of the age.

As they move to the garden, Jesus predicts that his followers will break the bond that they have celebrated at the meal. He announces that they will all fall away. But after he is raised from the dead, Jesus will restore the bond by going before the disciples into Galilee where they will see him (26:30–32). Jesus promises to be faithful despite the unfaithfulness of his followers. When Peter declares his special loyalty, Jesus predicts that Peter will deny him three times that very night. Peter protests that he will accept death before denying Jesus; the other disciples echo Peter's pledge of loyalty. Hearing this, the faithful in Matthew's community recall Jesus' predictions, the disciples' misunderstanding, and Jesus' instructions on the journey from Caesarea Philippi to Jerusalem (16:13–20:34).

Prayer in the Garden (26:36–46)

In the garden Jesus prays the Our Father, the prayer that he taught in the sermon on the mount (6:9–13). He withdraws from his disciples, then from Peter, James, and John. He urges them to watch and pray that they do not enter into temptation. Alone, Jesus asks that the cup of suffering might pass from him, but even more he submits to his Father's will. Finding his disciples asleep, Jesus rebukes Peter and then returns to pray again: "My Father, if this cannot pass unless I drink it, thy will be done!" He shuttles back to his disciples and then back to repeat the same words in prayer. Finally, Jesus returns to face his betrayal and arrest.

Jesus' passage through death to life—his end-time of tribulation—is about to begin. He expresses fear in the face of death, but he submits to whatever his suffering will cost because it is his Father's will, God's mysterious plan for saving the world. Struggling with death, Jesus asks to be delivered, but he remains faithful and obedient to his Father. As his followers sleep, he models how they are to watch and pray when they face the tribulations of their own end-time (24:1–25:46). Matthew's community finds strength and courage for their own struggles.

Arrest (26:47–56)

All that Jesus has predicted now begins to be fulfilled. Judas betrays him; the Jewish crowd from the chief priests and elders arrest him. Jesus acts quietly; they react with violence. In an intimate exchange, Judas kisses Jesus and salutes him: "Hail, Rabbi!" Jesus responds: "Friend, why are you here?" As the crowd moves to arrest Jesus, one of his disciples cuts off the ear of a slave of the high priest. Rebuking his follower, Jesus says that his arrest must take place as part of his Father's plan. Next, Jesus points out to the crowd the striking contrast between his calm, caring, healing presence to them in the temple and their agitated, violent actions in the garden. His disciples then run away, leaving Jesus alone with his enemies.

A dramatic contrast! As he speaks to Judas, to the disciple who wielded the sword, and to the crowds, Jesus remains calmly in charge of the situation. He accepts his death as his Father's will. Through the lens of the Hebrew scriptures, apparent failure and defeat become the carrying out of his God-given mission.

In this event, Matthew's community sees Jesus' predictions begin to be fulfilled (16:21; 17:22; 20:17–19; 26:1–2; 26:20–25). They also recall his victories against his enemies in the temple (21:1–23:39). Moreover, Jesus models his teaching in the sermon on the mount: "Do not resist one who is evil. . . . Love your enemies and pray for those who persecute you . . ." (5:38–48).

Jewish Trial and Peter's Denial (26:57–75)

Jesus spends the remainder of that night with the Jewish Sanhedrin at the home of Caiaphas the high priest, while Peter spends it outside with the Jewish maids and guards. In an informal session, Caiaphas and the Sanhedrin interrogate witnesses. Two witnesses cite Jesus' claim: "I am able to destroy the temple of God, and to rebuild it in three days" (26:61). But his enemies fail to build a case strong enough to put Jesus to death. The community at Antioch continues to think about Jesus' ministry in the temple (21:1–23:39) and his vision of the end-time (24:1–25:46).

With a solemn oath, Caiaphas next asks Jesus directly whether he is the Christ, the Son of God. Jesus answers that Caiaphas has indeed spoken the truth. He then continues by predicting that his enemies will see him as "the Son of Man seated at the right hand of Power, and coming on the clouds of heaven" (26:64). Because Jesus claims power for himself that is reserved to God, Caiaphas accuses him of blasphemy. Ironically the Jewish Sanhedrin condemns Jesus to death for being precisely the one whom the Jewish people hoped God would send to save them from Rome. Abusing Jesus, they spit in his face and strike him, while some slap him, saying, "Prophesy to us, you Christ! Who is it that struck you?" (27:68).

Meanwhile, other witnesses—a maid, a second maid, bystanders—interrogate Peter: "You also were with Jesus the Galilean" (27:69). Three times they accuse him; three times Peter denies any bond to Jesus: "I do not know the man" (27:74). A cock crows. Remembering Jesus' prediction, Peter repents and leaves Jesus' trial in bitter tears.

Reflecting on these trials of Jesus and Peter, Matthew's community again recalls the conversations between Jesus and Peter at Caesarea Philippi (16:13–28). When Jesus asked about himself, Peter responded: "You are the Christ, the Son of the living God." Now, when Caiaphas asks Jesus if he is the one Peter saw him to be, Jesus openly announces that he is the messiah. When Jesus predicted his suffering, death, and resurrection, Peter rebuked him, and Jesus called Peter "Satan." Now as those predictions come true, Peter denies any bond to the Jesus he professed to be the messiah. As Jesus instructed his followers at Caesarea, he described his coming in the glory of his Father's reign. Now, when he makes the same prediction to his enemies, they condemn him to death.

Peter models for Matthew's community the crisis that the threat of suffering can cause for those who choose to take up their cross and follow Jesus. But he also models hope. At the supper he called Jesus "Lord." On the way to the garden, he enthusiastically insisted that he would never deny his master. When he does deny him, he immediately recognizes what he has done and repents of his action with bitter tears. Because he continues to believe in Jesus, Peter chooses life even in his death-like denial. His faith—a little faith that is also afraid of suffering—includes the conviction that his repentance will lead to forgiveness. His tears remind the faithful at Antioch of Peter's dialogue with Jesus about forgiveness (18:21–35).

Judas' Death and Roman Trial (27:1–31)

Beginning with the Passover meal, this night ends at daybreak when the Sanhedrin issues its formal verdict against Jesus and takes him to Pilate, the Roman governor. Meanwhile Judas, recognizing what he has done, tries to free himself of being responsible for Jesus' blood. He returns the thirty pieces of silver to Jesus' enemies, saying, "I have sinned in betraying innocent blood" (27:4). When the chief priests and elders refuse to change their minds, Judas hangs himself. Questioning what to do with the blood-money, the Jewish authorities ironically decide to purchase a burial field for outcasts and strangers—the people whom Jesus healed during his ministry in Galilee (8:1–9:34).

As Peter models hope, so Judas models despair. Matthew's community remembers that Judas called Jesus "Rabbi" at the Passover meal. Now, they see that Judas' agreement with Jesus' enemies was also with the powers of evil, with Satan at work in those Jewish authorities. Judas chose to side with death. After his betrayal, he chose suicide rather than repentance. His example warns the Christians at Antioch against similar agreements with the Pharisees at Jamnia.

Next, Jesus stands trial before Pilate, the Roman governor. In a preliminary interrogation, Pilate asks Jesus if he is the long-awaited king whom the Jews expected to lead them in revolt against Rome. Jesus says that he is such a king. But when the chief priests and elders accuse him, Jesus remains silent. As he stumbles onto the truth about Jesus, Pilate is surprised at his silence.

Complying with the Passover custom, Pilate next offers the Jews a choice between Jesus Barabbas or Jesus called the Christ. As the Jews deliberate, Pilate's wife sends word about "that righteous man." Meanwhile, the chief priest and elders persuade the crowds to ask for Jesus Barabbas. When Pilate asks them again, the Jewish crowds side with Jesus' enemies, choose Barabbas, and demand that Jesus be crucified. When Pilate asks why, they shout all the more, "Let him be crucified" (27:23).

Pilate then washes his hands and says: "I am innocent of this man's blood; see to it yourselves" (27:24). All the Jewish people reinforce their fateful decision about Jesus by shouting, "His blood be on us and on our children" (27:25). With that, Pilate releases Barabbas. Having scourged Jesus, Pilate then delivers him to be crucified.

Next, Roman soldiers abuse Jesus in a mock coronation. The whole battalion dress him in a scarlet robe, place a crown of thorns on his head, and give him a reed for his scepter of power. They kneel to acclaim him by scornfully proclaiming, "Hail, King of the Jews" (27:29). Then they retract their salute by spitting on Jesus and striking him with the reed. Violent words and actions again meet a non-violent response. With supreme irony, Jesus is indeed king of the Jews precisely because he serves others by giving his life as their ransom (20:28).

Matthew's community knows that Israel rejects not only another prophet but their long-awaited messiah. In asking that Jesus be crucified, the Jewish authorities and crowds resemble their ancestors who rejected many prophets including Jeremiah at the time of exile. Now, Israel's choice marks another moment in the turbulent love-story between God and the chosen people. Again and again the Jews rejected God's forgiveness and faithful love. Now they reject God's messiah. As they watch this event, the Christians at Antioch recall Jesus' warnings in the temple against the Pharisees (21:1–23:39).

All the Jewish people cry that Jesus' blood be on their own generation and their children's generation. Matthew sees that their critical choice introduces the new and final age of God's reign. It brings God's harsh verdict and judgment against those two generations when they experienced the horrors of the Jewish revolt and the destruction of Jerusalem and the temple (A.D. 66–70). After that event, the reign of God moves away from the lost sheep of the house of Israel to include both Jews and Gentiles throughout the world (28:16–20).

Reflection Questions

- What does the eucharist mean to you? What would you like it to mean?
- What surfaces in you when you hear the word *suffering?* Do these events give you courage and strength?
- Have you ever felt betrayed or denied? How did you respond?
- Who models hope in our world? Who models despair?
- Do you think Israel's cry for Jesus' blood is a brand that has marked all Jews throughout history?

Reading

For a masterful treatment of the passion narrative read D. Senior, *The Passion of Jesus in the Gospel of Matthew.* Wilmington: Michael Glazier, 1985.

16

Passover Meal, Passion, Death and Resurrection (27:32–28:20)

Crucifixion and Death (27:32–56)

Events now move with haste to the crucifixion and death of Jesus. Simon of Cyrene literally takes up Jesus' cross. God's Son is crucified at Golgotha outside Jerusalem, that is, outside the vineyard of the Lord (21:39). Jesus drinks wine, a mild narcotic, to help deaden the pain. Matthew pays no attention to how Jesus was crucified. Instead, the evangelist mentions Jesus' garments and the Roman soldiers who keep the death watch. The public charge that Jesus is king of the Jews ironically contrasts with his death among robbers.

Matthew carefully describes taunts directed at Jesus by passersby. These onlookers include the people who cried for Jesus' crucifixion at the Roman trial. Their words recall the charges made against Jesus. Next, the chief priests with the scribes and elders—the Sanhedrin reassembled—also taunt Jesus by sneering, "He saved others; he cannot save himself. He is king of Israel; let him come down now from the cross, and we will believe in him. He trusts in God; let God deliver him now, if he desires him; for he said, I am the Son of God" (27:41–44). Matthew's community recalls that Jesus' name means he will save his people from their sins (1:20–21) and remembers that Satan used similar words to taunt Jesus in the desert (4:1–11). His commitment to his Father continues to be the issue between Jesus and his enemies, who are allies of Satan. Jesus' fidelity again proves to be more powerful than the forces of evil.

Jesus' death anticipates the end of the age (24:29–31). As darkness covers the earth, Jesus cries out in pain, "My God, my God, why hast thou forsaken me?" (Ps 22:1). When the soldiers mention Elijah, Matthew's listeners remember John the Baptist. With another cry, Jesus yields up his spirit. For the Antioch community, his final act of obedience must recall Jesus' actions at the Passover meal (26:26–29) and his prayer in the garden (26:36–46).

Awesome signs of cosmic power immediately announce God's answer both to Jesus' cries and to the taunts of his enemies. The curtain of the temple is torn from top to bottom. This curtain hung before the holy of holies to mark the place where the people of Israel stood in reverence before their God who was present in the place where the ark of the covenant, the menorah, and the manna were preserved. The earth shakes, rocks split, and tombs open —all to anticipate both Jesus' resurrection (28:2–3) and his return as triumphant Son of Man (24:29–31). Jesus' death reveals the new age of God's reign. John announced it at the Jordan; Jesus revealed it by his words and actions in Galilee and Jerusalem. God's reign will be fully established only when Jesus returns in glory as the triumphant Son of Man.

A Roman centurion and the soldiers keeping the death watch had mocked Jesus. Now, seeing these events, they announce, "Truly this was the Son of God" (27:54). Women who followed Jesus from Galilee and the unnamed woman at Bethany witness the events from afar. Gentile soldiers model faith; women remain faithful to the end. Matthew's community is surprised that Peter and the other men who followed Jesus from the start do not witness the signs at his death.

Psalm 22 plays in the background of the crucifixion: "My God, my God why hast though forsaken me? (1) . . . In thee our fathers trusted; they trusted, and thou didst deliver them (4) . . . All who see me mock at me, they make mouths at me, they wag their heads (7) . . . I can count all my bones—they stare and gloat over me; they divide my garments among them, and for my raiment they cast lots (17–18)." In this psalm, however, faith follows anguish and desolation. The psalmist prays that God will vindicate the suffering just man and that all the ends of the earth will turn to the Lord. Matthew's community often prays this traditional Jewish prayer.

Burial; Women and Guards; Resurrection (27:57–28:10)

Another surprising disciple, a rich man named Joseph of Arimathea, risks giving an honorable burial to Jesus. Asking Pilate for the body of Jesus, Joseph buries it in his own new tomb and rolls a great stone to the door of the sepulchre. Like wise maidens, the women sit opposite the tomb, watching and waiting for the bridegroom's return (25:1–13). Meanwhile, Jesus' enemies continue their opposition by asking Pilate to guard the tomb. But Pilate refuses to use his own soldiers. Jewish, not Roman, soldiers watch with the women at the tomb.

After the Passover sabbath, the women return to continue their watch. (The woman at Bethany had already anointed Jesus body for burial.) More apocalyptic signs meet them. With another earthquake an angel of the Lord descends from heaven to roll back the stone. Appearing like lightning, the angel is robed in garments white as snow. Matthew's community recalls how Jesus looked at the transfiguration (17:1–8).

The Jewish soldiers, shaken with fear, become like dead men, unable to see or hear what follows. The angel announces, "Do not be afraid; for I know that you seek Jesus who was crucified. He is not here; for he has risen, as he said. Come, see the place where he lay. Then go quickly and tell his disciples that he has risen from the dead, and behold, he is going before you to Galilee; there you will see him. Lo, I have told you" (28:5–8). Those at Antioch who follow the risen Jesus must recall that he predicted both his resurrection and his return to Galilee. With a mixture of fear and joy, the women run to carry out the angel's command by taking the message of his resurrection to his male disciples.

On their way, the women experience the risen Jesus. After reassuring them, Jesus repeats the angel's command to tell his disciples that he goes before them into Galilee. In contrast, the Jewish guards report the empty tomb to Jesus' enemies. The chief priests and elders take final counsel against Jesus and bribe the guards to say that his disciples came during the night to steal Jesus' body. As Jesus' enemies continue their hostility, the women model resurrection faith. The Christians at Antioch understand that the conflict with the Pharisees continues.

Great Commission in Galilee (28:16–20)

Acting on the message received from the women, the eleven disciples return to Galilee. Here Jesus preached the gospel of the kingdom to Israel, taught in the Jewish synagogues, and healed every disease and every infirmity (4:23; 9:35; 11:1). Now the risen Jesus appears to his disciples. Still men of little faith, some show him homage and worship him while others doubt.

Jesus reveals that he now sits at the right hand of Power: "All authority in heaven and on earth has been given to me" (28:18). Now that he is risen, the power that was limited to the lost sheep of the house of Israel during his earthly life extends to all creation. With such universal power, Jesus next commissions the eleven: "Go therefore and make disciples of all nations, baptizing them in the name of the Father and of the Son and of the Holy Spirit, teaching them to observe all that I have commanded you" (28:19–20). His new status as their risen Lord means that his disciples' mission now extends beyond Israel to include both Jews and Gentiles throughout the world. He entrusts to them his universal power. Finally, Jesus promises, "And lo, I am with you always to the end of the age" (28:20). Jesus—Emmanuel, God-with-us (1:21)—will be identified with his eleven disciples in their universal mission, as he was in their limited mission to Israel (10:40–42).

What an incredible turn of events! What an act of trust in these eleven men! A new beginning! A new mission until the end of the age! Matthew's community remembers well that Jesus chose these men to share his mission to the lost sheep of the house of Israel (9:35–10:42) and that he also predicted that Judas would betray him, that Peter would deny him, and that the rest would be scattered at the moment of his arrest (26:30–35). They all did what Jesus predicted. But in spite of their failure, the risen Jesus now entrusts to these same men the universal mission to the new and true Israel. Risen, Jesus can no longer walk with them on that mission. He can only work in and through their activities of baptizing and teaching what he has taught them. Now all depends on their fidelity in carrying out this new call to let God's reign work through them to save both Jews and Gentiles. The Jews and Gentiles in Antioch find deep meaning in this final commission.

With this event, Matthew ends his story about Jesus. Within the story all that Jesus predicted has taken place except his words about his return in glory. Matthew's community remembers that Jesus first spoke of that end-time in parables about wheat and weeds and about a fish net full of good and bad fish (13:24–30, 36–43, 47–50). They recall how Jesus also instructed his disciples and warned his enemies that they would see him return as the triumphant Son of Man (16:24–28; 26:59–68) and how he told stories about the judgment of both his disciples and the nations (24:45–25:46). Describing his return to the Jewish Sanhedrin, Jesus said, "Hereafter you will see the Son of Man seated at the right hand of Power, and coming on the clouds of heaven" (26:64).

As Matthew's community ponders Jesus' final commission, they can be confident that as all his other predictions have taken place, so Jesus' predictions about his return at the end of the age will come true. No one can know the day or the hour of their fulfillment. But the risen Jesus calls the faithful at Antioch to live in hope, that is, to choose life even in their death-like, uncertain times. Jesus will be faithful to them, even when they are unfaithful to Jesus. He has predicted that they will know persecution and tribulation, mutual betrayal and hatred, even that their love will grow cold. Again his predictions have been fulfilled. But the community must now focus on that other prediction: "And this gospel of the kingdom will be preached throughout the whole world, as a testimony to all nations; and then the end will come" (24:14).

Reflection Questions

- How do you respond to the death of Jesus and its aftermath? Spend time with your response.
- With whom do you identify—the Roman soldiers, the women, the absent men disciples?
- Pray Psalm 22. How does it touch your life?
- How do you respond to the risen Jesus? How do you understand his resurrection? How would you explain it to someone who asked?
- Does the final commission give you hope? How might it provide some direction in these uncertain times?

CONCLUSION

Good News for Uncertain Times

Matthew's story about Jesus did not provide solutions to the problems that his community faced in their uncertain times. Nor does it provide answers to the issues we are addressing in ours. Many contemporary fundamentalists attempt to find clear answers from his story, but we know that the insights from this gospel cannot substitute for our moral decisions or dictate our actions. On the other hand, some historians consider Matthew's story so ancient that it can tell us nothing about how we are to approach life in our modern world. Again we disagree, since we believe that the word of God can be universally applied.

We have respected both the historical distance in time and the differences in culture that separate us from Matthew and from his community. Still, we have listened deeply to the evangelist's story to discover what the struggle to believe in Jesus Christ and to live that faith in uncertain times means. Matthew's story carries a vision of the human condition that provides us with a stance toward life, a way to view the world in which we live. We pray and study the story to assimilate its vision and to integrate the values, attitudes, and convictions that arise from that vision. We do not expect the story to give us strategies for concrete action in our unique historical situation. Although Matthew's story cannot directly shape our decisions, it *can* shape us—the decision makers.

Matthew's vision urges his community and urges us to let these values inform our lives. He encourages us with the following invitations: Recall your roots! Delay gratification! Deepen your faith! Grow in love! Wait with patience! Become like children! Lament your losses! Lead by serving! Go out to the nations! Choose life! Matthew highlights these themes, because he wants his story to show how Christians are to recover their past, face the reality of their present uncertain times, and move with conviction into the future.

Recall Your Roots!

Matthew begins his story with a list of names in which he traces the lineage of Jesus from Abraham to David, from David to the exile, and from the exile to Joseph, the father of Jesus.

> The book of the genealogy of Jesus Christ, the son of David, the son of Abraham. Abraham was the father of Isaac, and Isaac the father of Jacob, and Jacob the father of Judah and his brothers. . . . And David was the father of Solomon by the wife of Uriah, and Solomon the father of Rehoboam, and Rehoboam the father of Abijah. . . . And after the deportation to Babylon; Jechoniah was the father of Shealtiel, and Shealtiel the father of Zerubbabel, and Zerubbabel the father of Abiud . . . and Jacob the father of Joseph the husband of Mary, of whom Jesus was born, who is called Christ. So all the generations from Abraham to David were fourteen generations, and from David

to the deportation to Babylon fourteen generations, and from the deportation to Babylon to the
Christ fourteen generations (1:1–17).

In this passage, Matthew shows how Jesus is rooted
both in Abraham, the father of the Jews, and in David, the
king from whom the messiah must descend. He also recalls
the exile, perhaps the most uncertain time in Israel's history. Since his community in Antioch is rooted in Jesus, it
is also rooted in Israel. Indeed, these followers of Jesus are
members of the true messianic Israel. Their experiences
remind them of Israel in exile. God promised Abraham
that through him all the nations would be blessed.
Matthew ends his story with Jesus fulfilling that promise
by sending his followers to make disciples of all the nations
(28:16–20).

How do we, as individuals, families and communities,
understand our roots? How might we recall and order our
genealogy? What light would such a family tree throw on
the present? How would we divide the time? How might
that process give us a sense of being rooted, as we face our
own uncertain times? Since Alex Haley published *Roots,*
many families have traced their roots, and many communities have retold stories about their founders. That may be
why we are interested in Matthew's story of Jesus.

Delay Gratification!

Matthew's Jesus begins his extensive teaching with
beatitudes that name the values, attitudes, and dispositions of those who repent and believe the good news about
the reign of God.

Blessed are the poor in spirit, for theirs is the
kingdom of heaven. Blessed are those who mourn,

for they shall be comforted. Blessed are the meek, for they shall inherit the earth. Blessed are those who hunger and thirst for righteousness, for they shall be satisfied. Blessed are the merciful, for they shall obtain mercy. Blessed are the pure in heart, for they shall see God. Blessed are the peacemakers, for they shall be called children of God. Blessed are those who are persecuted for righteousness' sake, for theirs is the kingdom of heaven (5:3–10).

Knowing that they need God, Jesus' followers desire that God be the center of their lives. Hence they are happy now, because their reward will be great in heaven. How would we add to these beatitudes? Might we say today: "Blessed are those who see the pain in our world, for they will share in its joy. Blessed are those who let themselves feel anxious, for anxiety will lead them to know what is right. Blessed are the compassionate, for they will be treated with compassion."

Deepen Your Faith!

Matthew's Jesus often challenges his followers to deepen the "little faith" that they exhibit during a storm at sea. According to Matthew:

When Jesus got into the boat, his disciples followed him. And behold, there arose a great storm on the sea, so that the boat was being swamped by the waves; but he was asleep. And they went and woke him, saying, "Save us, Lord; we are perishing." And he said to them, "Why are you afraid, O men of little faith?" Then he rose and rebuked the

winds and the sea; and there was a great calm.
And the men marveled, saying, "What sort of
man is this, that even winds and sea obey him?"
(8:23–27).

Thus, the followers of Jesus trust him enough to risk
getting into the boat with him to cross the treacherous lake
at night. Confronted by the real dangers of the storm, they
panic with their faith dissolving into fear of death.
Matthew invites his community to deepen their faith in
Jesus, as they experience panic because of Nero's persecution and the developments within Judaism since the revolt
against Rome.

We reflect on this event at critical moments in our
own storm at sea. Do we have enough faith to risk getting
into the boat with Jesus? Do we want such faith? Do we
realize that he is with us, even though asleep? Do we panic
when Jesus' failure to intervene on our behalf seems to
imply a lack of concern? We may want to cry, "Save us,
Lord; can't you see that we are perishing?" We may hear
his rebuke: "Why do you doubt? In this storm I invite you
to a deeper faith, a deeper trust in my love for you and in
my power over the storm." How do we respond to his words
and actions? How might we be open to that deeper faith?

Grow in Love!

In the temple at Jerusalem, Matthew's Jesus confronts the Pharisees who interpret the law for the Jews.
The Pharisees test him with a series of questions aimed at
putting him on the horns of a dilemma. But each time
Jesus thwarts them with a statement or a counter-ques-

tion. Finally they ask about the greatest commandment in the law.

> When the Pharisees heard that he had silenced the Sadducees, they came together. And one of them, a lawyer, asked him a question, to test him. "Teacher, which is the great commandment in the law?" And he said to him, "You shall love the Lord your God with all your heart, and with all your soul, and with all your mind. This is the great and first commandment. And a second is like it, You shall love your neighbor as yourself. On these two commandments depend all the law and the prophets" (22:34–40).

Thus, Jesus weaves love of God, love of self, and love of neighbor into one single commandment. According to Jesus, the law and the prophets, that is, the entire Hebrew scriptures, rest on these three dimensions of love. Matthew urges his community to focus on this spiritual foundation so that their love may not continue to grow cold.

Love is still that all-embracing value for Christians. We cannot love God without loving ourselves and our neighbors. We cannot truly love ourselves without loving our neighbors and God. We cannot love our neighbors well without loving ourselves and God. Matthew invites us to ask how we can grow in love for God, for others, for ourselves, for our world. What stands in the way? How might God want to lead us to that deeper love?

Become Like Children!

Matthew's Jesus instructs his disciples that they are to become like children.

At that time the disciples came to Jesus, saying,
"Who is the greatest in the kingdom of heaven?"
And calling to him a child, he put him in the midst
of them, and said, "Truly, I say to you, unless you
turn and become like children, you will never
enter the kingdom of heaven. Whoever humbles
himself like this child, he is the greatest in the
kingdom of heaven" (18:1–4).

This is another crucial lesson for Matthew's community. Instead of living with grandiose dreams about sharing
political power and glory, true followers must become like
children. They must be simple and open, honest and trusting, creative and playful. Matthew urges the faithful in
Antioch to live as little ones, so as to be great in the kingdom of heaven.

Can we take these words seriously in our own adult
world? Possibly Matthew's community can become like
children. But how can we live as children in today's complex society? How do well-educated, sophisticated adults
become like children? How can we recover the child's qualities in our adult lives? Does our world call us to recover
those qualities?

Wait with Patience!

Matthew's Jesus tells his followers and the crowds a
story about wheat and weeds.

The kingdom of heaven may be compared to a
man who sowed good seed in his field: but while
men were sleeping, his enemy came and sowed
weeds among the wheat, and went away. So when
the plants came up and bore grain, the weeds ap-

peared also. And the servants of the householder came and said to him, "Sir, did you not sow good seed in your field? How then has it weeds?" He said to them, "An enemy has done this." The servants said to him, "Then do you want us to go and gather them?" But he said, "No; lest in gathering the weeds you root up the wheat along with them. Let both grow together until the harvest; and at harvest time I will tell the reapers, gather the weeds first and bind them in bundles to be burned, but gather the wheat into my barn" (13:24–30).

In this parable, Jesus compares the kingdom of heaven to the situation close to his hearers. A householder sows good wheat seeds in his field. But his enemy secretly and maliciously sows with the wheat a poisonous weed. As their sprouts push up out of the ground, darnel looks like wheat, but later is recognized as a weed. Servants report to the householder. He surprises them by telling them not to attempt to pull the weeds but to wait until harvest time. Then they will separate the two, tie the weeds into bundles to be burned as fuel, and gather the wheat into his barns. For now the servants are to let wheat and weeds grow together, as they watch and wait with patience for the harvest. Matthew wants his community to imitate the servants.

How do we respond to this story? Where do we find wheat and weeds growing together in ourselves and in our communities, in our nation and in the world? What does letting them grow together while we wait with patience for the harvest mean? Are we not to respond to the challenges of our times? Are we not to work to create a better world?

Lament Your Losses!

After Matthew's Jesus confronts his enemies in the
temple, he warns them about their ways and then laments
over Jerusalem.

> O Jerusalem, Jerusalem, killing the prophets and
> stoning those who are sent to you! How often
> would I have gathered your children together as a
> hen gathers her brood under her wings, and you
> would not! Behold, your house is forsaken and
> desolate. For I tell you, you will not see me again,
> until you say "Blessed is he who comes in the
> name of the Lord" (23:37–39).

Listening to Jesus' lament, Matthew's community can
identify with its pathos. The holy city had been an evil city.
Jewish religious authorities had persecuted Jesus, their
founder, and then the community of apostles from which
their community in Antioch was founded. After the
Romans destroyed both city and temple, Pharisees continued that persecution through decrees from Jamnia.

Matthew invites us to name our losses, to enter the
pain of loss, and to lament with Jesus, so that we may move
beyond our losses to new life. Anger, sadness, sorrow, and
compassion name feelings that many of us carry but may
be afraid to express. How are we called to name our losses,
to let ourselves be angry and feel sad, to express our sorrow
to each other, so that we may find a compassion that will
move us to create a better world?

Lead by Serving!

As Jesus approaches Jerusalem, the mother of James
and John begs for special privileges for her two sons. The

two disciples vow that they can drink from the cup that Jesus is about to consume. Matthew then recounts the reaction of the other disciples and Jesus' instructions:

> When the ten heard it, they were indignant at the two brothers. But Jesus called them to him and said, "You know that the rulers of the Gentiles lord it over them, and their great men exercise authority over them. It shall not be so among you; but whoever would be great among you must be your servant, and whoever would be first among you must be your slave, even as the Son of Man came not to be served but to serve, and to give his life as a ransom for many" (20:24–28).

Thus, paradox is at the heart of Jesus' teaching—the paradox in his own journey through suffering to glory, the paradox in his instructions that his followers are to take up their cross and follow him, to find their life by losing it, to become first by being last, and to exercise leadership by serving others as the slaves of all. His way and theirs is through suffering to glory, through humiliation to exaltation, through death to life.

Paradox, which suggests the possibilities in an apparent contradiction, proposes something opposed to common sense, a reversal of ordinary logic, a world upside down, a violation of our normal instincts. Jesus' paradoxical statements catch us unawares; they shock and startle us. By setting up a conflict with our usual way of perceiving reality and of finding meaning in our lives, paradox enables us to see possibilities where previously we saw none. Reason alone cannot explain a paradox. It invites us to view life not as unreasonable, but as beyond reason, that is, as profoundly mysterious.

Based on daily experience, common sense tells us that

leaders give orders and followers obey, that leaders often behave arrogantly toward the persons under their authority, whether in families, in the workplace, or in church and society. The paradox of servant-leaders contradicts, even offends, those expectations. How are we to hear these instructions? Can we take them seriously? Has servant-leadership ever worked in our society? Can it work today? Can this paradox lead us to see new possibilities in our uncertain times? We may need to risk trying to live the paradox that Jesus teaches.

Go Out to the Nations!

In the last event in Matthew's gospel, Jesus appears to his eleven disciples as their risen Lord.

> Now the eleven disciples went to Galilee to the mountain to which Jesus had directed them. And when they saw him, they worshiped him, but some doubted. And Jesus came and said to them, "All authority in heaven and on earth has been given to me. Go, therefore, and make disciples of all nations, baptizing them in the name of the Father, and of the Son, and of the Holy Spirit, teaching them to observe all that I have commanded you; and lo, I am with you always to the close of the age" (28:16–20).

This final commission is the climax of Matthew's story. Now that Jesus has come into full authority over heaven and earth, he sends his disciples on a universal mission to both Jews and Gentiles. No longer with them on earth, Jesus entrusts the continuation of his mission to the men who had run away from him in the garden at the time of his arrest. The ultimate success of his work for God's reign now depends entirely upon them. Matthew calls his mixed community at Antioch to this universal mission.

Aware of the Lord's presence with us, how are we to hear this commission? What does making disciples of all nations mean? How do we translate this task into concrete action in our everyday lives? We may want to respond, but how are we to do so as individuals and communities of Christians? What is our mission in these uncertain times? Do we want to formulate a mission-statement for ourselves as individuals, for our various communities—our families, our work world, our parish, our religious community, our church, our neighborhood, our nation?

Choose Life!

Matthew's Jesus describes his second coming to his disciples:

> Immediately after the tribulation of those days the sun will be darkened, and the moon will not give its light, and the stars will fall from heaven, and the powers of the heavens will be shaken; then will appear the sign of the Son of Man in heaven, and then all the tribes of the earth will mourn, and they will see the Son of Man coming on the clouds of heaven with power and great glory; and he will send out his angels with a loud trumpet call, and they will gather his elect from the four winds, from one end of heaven to the other (24:29–31).

This vision of the future is meant to sustain the disciples, as they walk the way of Jesus through suffering to glory. Jesus assures his followers that joy is more ultimate than suffering, God's power more ultimate than human weakness, life more ultimate than death.

When we hope, we are enabled by God to choose life even in death-like situations. When we despair, we let death exercise its power. Hope happens when we choose life over death. We experience hope as a power that can lift us out of the clutches of pain, so that we may see in the pain the seeds of new possibilities. Hopeful feelings or sensible consolation may not always accompany hope. But hope empowers us to wait in uncertain times for new life to happen in and through the suffering that we are called to experience. Hope enables us to rely on a power greater than suffering or death. With faith and love, hope is an energy for daily Christian living. With these energies we create the images of the future that influence how we live in the present.

Our lives today are a story that we are writing with our words and actions. We shape our lives by weaving together a number of stories. We inherit some stories from our background—Irish Catholics, German Lutherans, United States citizens. Other stories we freely choose. We decide to be spouse or parent, plumber or nurse, member of this church or that organization. Our challenge is to weave several stories together into a tapestry that is both true and meaningful.

Matthew offers us a master-story about God's reign. We can let this tale become the wider landscape for the other stories by which we choose to live. The good news can flow together with other stories, like streams that form a single river. Matthew's story about Jesus calls for a commitment, a change of heart, a new trust, a deeper love. This love will play itself out not only in our families and our church but also in all that makes up our everyday lives. The themes we have teased out of Matthew's story can be decisive for us who want to believe in Jesus Christ. They can shape the deepest desires that inform our values and attitudes, our intentions and convictions. These, in turn, influence how we make decisions about what is right and wrong, how we channel our creative energy into the concrete tasks that need doing.

Matthew's story of Jesus offers us a hopeful vision for these uncertain times. It is a perennial Christian vision that in each age invites us to find again the treasure hidden in the field or the pearl of great price. Matthew's gospel invites us to understand and live the mystery of the reign of God.

Epilogue

Using This Book

This book offers a process to lead readers to pray with and study Matthew's gospel. What follows is a suggestion for how adult groups might come together to reflect, discuss, and pray with both the gospel and this book.

1. Leadership and Group Size

Leaders provide support by facilitating the discussion and prayer sessions. They *enable* the discussion rather than instruct or teach. Leaders share their own reflections, feelings, and questions; they *model* this process for the other participants.

Because the sharing of the group will reflect both the needs of the particular group and the leader's personal style, the leader will want to be thoroughly familiar with the material before meeting with the participants. In the first few sessions the group will find its own comfort level and way of proceeding.

Leaders are also responsible for a suitable, comfortable meeting place—a home, a pleasant room in the parish complex. If participants are to maintain contact and continue to feel wanted and included in the group, leaders must call members who have missed a meeting to communicate the next meeting date and the assigned preparation.

About twelve participants is the recommended size, so that members may come to know and trust each other more than superficially. This size promotes a sense of *collective giftedness* with each person being able to see what he or she is able to contribute to the group process.

2. Length of Meeting

Each meeting should be planned for between one and a half and two hours. This allows time for reflection, sharing, reaction, prayer, and evaluation. *Before* the meeting time, participants need to read the assigned sections of both Matthew's gospel and this book. If possible, they should also reflect on the questions for discussion.

The meeting time needs to be consistent. A fixed time creates a climate in which study can lead to prayer and prayer to study. The group can meet weekly for ten weeks or twice a month for five months or once a month for ten months.

The following schedule will help the group move easily through the book:

1st Week—Prologue/Chapter 1
2nd Week—Chapter 2
3rd Week—Chapters 3–4
4th Week—Chapters 5–6
5th Week—Chapters 7–8
6th Week—Chapters 9–10
7th Week—Chapters 11–12

8th Week—Chapters 13–14
9th Week—Chapters 15–16
10th Week—Conclusion

A six-week module seems hasty but possible:

1st Week—Prologue/Chapters 1–2
2nd Week—Chapters 3–4
3rd Week—Chapters 5–6–7–8
4th Week—Chapters 9–10–11–12
5th Week—Chapters 13–14–15–16
6th Week—Conclusion

3. Prayer

Praying with Matthew's gospel is integral to the group process. Participants need to actually pray rather than merely read about praying. Within the sessions, the group may want to spend some time together in prayer. Scripture-sharing is a good method.

Participants profit by making a simple contract with each other that expresses their serious commitment both to each other and to God. They agree to do the following:

- pray faithfully with Matthew's gospel each day for a period that each one chooses—perhaps fifteen or twenty minutes;
- record their prayer experience for sharing with the group;
- spend a few minutes sharing their prayer experience with the group.

All participants are invited to record their prayer experience in the way that suits them best. Some may want to draw freely with pencils or crayons. Their concern is that the simple design expresses what happened in their prayer, not that their drawing be excellent art. Others may want to write simple notes, not even sentences, that will remind them of what struck them in prayer. Others may want to write more freely in a journal to articulate their thoughts and feelings. Still others may want to talk about their prayer with their spouse or a friend.

4. Evaluation

Toward the end of each session, the leader should ask each member of the group what he or she found to be new, insightful, helpful, affirming, or disturbing in the session. The leader then reminds the participants about the time and place of the next meeting and about the assigned material. The leader may also want to encourage the members to continue praying each day and recording their prayer experience.

Readings

For a fine presentation of the current movement toward intentional Christian communities see B.J. Lee and M.A. Cowan, *Dangerous Memories: House Churches and Our American Story* (Sheed and Ward, 1986).

Selected Bibliography

Commentaries

Fenton, J.C., *Saint Matthew*. Philadelphia: Westminster, 1978.

Harrington, D.J., *Matthew*. Collegeville: Liturgical Press, 1983.

Meier, J.P., *Matthew*. Wilmington: Michael Glazier, 1980.

Meier, J.P., *Matthew*. New York: William H. Sadlier, 1983.

Schweizer, E., *The Good News According to Matthew*. Atlanta: John Knox Press, 1975.

Senior, D., *Invitation to Matthew*. Garden City: Doubleday, 1971.

Studies

Bornkamm, G., G. Barth, H.J. Held, *Tradition and Interpretation in Matthew*. London: SCM Press, 1982.

Crosby, M.H., *Spirituality of the Beatitudes*. Maryknoll: Orbis Books, 1981.

Davies, W.D., *The Setting of the Sermon on the Mount*.

New York/London: Cambridge University Press, 1964.

Davies, W.D., *The Sermon on the Mount.* New York/London: Cambridge University Press, 1969.

Edwards, R.A., *Matthew's Story of Jesus.* Philadelphia: Fortress Press, 1985.

Ellis, P., *Matthew: His Mind and His Message.* Collegeville: Liturgical Press, 1974.

Kingsbury, J.D., *Matthew: Structure, Christology, Kingdom.* Philadelphia: Fortress Press, 1975.

Kingsbury, J.D., *Matthew.* Philadelphia: Fortress Press, 1977.

Kingsbury, J.D., *Matthew as Story.* Philadelphia: Fortress Press, 1986.

Kunkel, F., *Creation Continues.* Mahwah: Paulist Press, 1987.

Lambrecht, J., *The Sermon on the Mount.* Wilmington: Michael Glazier, 1986.

Senior, D., *Matthew: A Gospel for the Church.* Chicago: Franciscan Herald Press, 1973.

Senior, D., *The Passion of Jesus in the Gospel of Matthew.* Wilmington: Michael Glazier, 1985.

Stendahl, K., *The School of St. Matthew and Its Use of the Old Testament.* Philadelphia: Fortress Press, 1968.

Thompson, W.G., *Matthew's Advice for a Divided Community—Mt 17:22–18:35.* Rome: Biblical Institute Press, 1970.

White, R.E.O. *The Mind of Matthew.* Philadelphia: Westminster Press, 1979.